The Federal Trust for Education and Research

The Federal Trust's aim is to enlighten public debate on federal issues of national, continental and global government. It does this in the light of its statutes which state that it shall promote 'studies in the principles of international relations, international justice and supranational government.'

The Trust conducts enquiries, promotes seminars and conferences and publishes reports, books and teaching materials.

The Trust is the UK member of the Trans-European Policy Studies Association (TEPSA), a grouping of fifteen think tanks from Member States of the European Union.

Up-to-date information about the Federal Trust's publications and projects can be found at **www.fedtrust.co.uk**

The Federal Trust is a Registered Charity No. 272241
Dean Bradley House, 52 Horseferry Road,
London SW1P 2 AF
Company Limited by Guarantee No. 1269848

Marketing and distribution by Kogan Page Ltd
Printed by J W Arrowsmith Ltd

to Christine
and for Katharine, who understands

Contents

Our Contributors

Roger Beetham (Editor). Retired diplomat. Spokesman of the Ministerial team negotiating Britain's entry into the European Community (1970-71), and later of Roy Jenkins as President of the European Commission (1977-81). Ambassador to the Council of Europe in Strasbourg 1993-97.

Simon Buckby is Campaign Director of Britain in Europe.

Janet Bush has been Director of New Europe, the cross-party campaign supporting Britain's membership of the EU but opposing membership of the Euro, since March 1999. Previous career in journalism, finally Economics Editor of *The Times*.

Bill Cash, Conservative MP for Stafford, then Stone, since 1984. Chairman of the European Foundation, a consistent opponent of Britain in Europe.

David Clark was Special Adviser to Robin Cook from1994 to 2001, including his tenure as Foreign Secretary

Sir Roy Denman was a member of the team negotiating British entry into the EC (1970-71), then principal British negotiator in successive international trade rounds, before joining the European Commission in 1977 as Director of External Relations, and becoming EC Ambassador in Washington (1982-89).

John Edmonds has been General Secretary of the GMB since 1986.

Nigel Farage was elected to the European Parliament as a Member for the Southeast of England from the UK Independence Party in 1999.

Christopher Huhne, a professional journalist, was elected Liberal Democrat Member of the European Parliament, also from the Southeast of England, in 1999.

Neil Kinnock, Labour MP from 1970-95, was Leader of the Party 1983-1992. Member of the EC Commission since 1995, becoming Vice-President in 2000.

Ruth Lea, a former Economic Adviser to the government and the private banking sector, has been Director of Policy at the Institute of Directors since 1995.

Ken Livingstone, former Leader of the Greater London Council (1981-86) and Labour Member of Parliament (1987-2001), was elected Mayor of London in 2000.

John Stevens is leader of the Pro-Euro Conservative Party. He was Conservative member of the European Parliament from 1989 - 1999.

Lord Shore of Stepney, a Labour MP from 1964-97, was a Cabinet Minister in both Harold Wilson's and James Callaghan's Governments (1967-70 and 1974-79). One of the consistent leaders of the Anti-Market campaign.

Lord Simon of Highbury spent 34 years in BP, becoming Managing Director in 1986 (until 1995). He was Minister of State at the Treasury for two years in Tony Blair's first Government.

Ernest Wistrich, CBE, was Director of the European Movement from 1969 to 1986 and principal organiser of the pro-European forces in the 1975 Referendum.

Robert Worcester is Chairman of MORI, London, having previously being Managing Director.

Introduction by the Editor

Roger Beetham

When people discover that I spent much of my diplomatic career involved with Europe, and in particular was the press spokesman of the team which negotiated Britain's membership of the European Communities in 1970-72, and then acted as Roy Jenkins' spokesman in Brussels when he was President of the Commission at the end of the 70s, many of them say 'ah, you never came clean with us at that time, not even in the Referendum, about the political implications of membership.'

I do not actually think it is true, but it remains the case that a very large number of people believe it to be so. This belief therefore becomes a factor, every bit as powerful as a fact, which has to be taken into account in the debate about the implications of sterling joining the Euro, of British membership of the single currency.

I do not personally agree with those who play down the political arguments (whether for or against) because the political implications are extremely important, indeed vital. To this extent I agree with the sceptics and opponents that the issue must be the subject of a full and deep debate. It is vital that this time, whatever the outcome, the 'People are Persuaded' – one way or the other – and that no-one should again be able to claim 'you never came clean with us.'

Constitutionally, I have always been sceptical as to whether the Referendum has a place in our essentially parliamentary political system, but I have become entirely persuaded of its necessity in the case of the Euro debate for two reasons: one just given – the need to settle the argument, if possible once and for all; the other (which I think the 2001 General Election campaign vindicated) the need to separate the issue from the election of a government. Particularly if one major party is split on the issue, the arguments become distorted and mixed up with others, so there is not the clear concentration on the implications of the issue of Britain and the single European currency which its importance to our country's future warrants.

The Federal Trust and I hope that these articles, representing a cross-section of views on the subject, will be a contribution to the debate and the task of 'Persuading the People' – not one way or the other, but that all the implications must be weighed and a conclusion reached on the basis of as wide a discussion as possible. We do not at all dismiss the economic arguments, but for us the political considerations are crucial, so that the focus of the majority of contributions to this book is political. I have tried to order the articles so that the book takes the form of something of a debate, representing all its aspects. To this end I have linked them with a commentary, also to help guide the reader along.

Apart from trying to encourage comparative brevity, I have not interpreted my editorial role in any interventionist sense, so all contributions are left as the authors have wished. The articles have been written especially for this book.

I am grateful to all the contributors for their time and co-operation, particularly as they all gave their services free, and to the Federal Trust for inviting me to edit this volume.

Chapter 1

The British:
Reluctant Europeans

Robert M. Worcester

Editor's Commentary

*To set the scene, **Bob Worcester**, doyen of pollsters, describes the challenge facing those whose task in 'Persuading the People' is to swing a still sceptical majority of public opinion to a favourable view of joining the single European currency, especially faced with the uncertainty of the Government's position on timing of a referendum. We have nevertheless decided that this contribution to the Euro debate should be launched early on, in the hope that the proponents will be encouraged to press, and the sceptics to see the arguments, for an early decision. Either way, British interests are not likely to be advanced by more delay.*

The British: Reluctant Europeans

Robert M. Worcester[1]

I do not believe that in the life of this Parliament, 2001-2005, the Prime Minister will find it politically expedient to join in the Single European Currency, no matter the outcome of the so-called 'five economic tests.'

The Foreign Policy Centre published a booklet[2] in July 2000 in which I forecast that the Blair Government would call the promised referendum on British entry into the Single European Currency in November, 2001, and win it, just. My forecast was based on the nearly half of the British who say either 'I am generally in favour of British entry into the Single European Currency, but I could be persuaded to vote against it if I thought it was in Britain's economic interests to do so,' or 'I am generally opposed to British entry into the Single European Currency, but I could be persuaded to vote for it if I thought it was in Britain's economic interests to do so.'

I thought then that with the concerted support of the Prime Minister and the Chancellor, the majority of big business and the City, significant trade union support and both the Labour Party and the Liberal Democrats joined by the 'big beasts' of the Conservative Party, Ken Clarke and Michael Heseltine, the public could be persuaded to learn to love the Euro, or at least sufficient of them to give the nod to the Referendum question on the Euro.

After the loss of confidence in the Prime Minister and the Chancellor in the Autumn of 2000, I reconsidered my forecast, and said that the Referendum could not be won with confidence, and therefore would not be called, in the life of the next Parliament. Yet by nearly four to one the British say they want Britain to be at the 'heart of Europe.'

The likeliest outcome of the next election is a narrow win for Labour, either independent of the Liberal Democrats, or in conjunction with them; either way, Labour will need the LibDems for the following Parliament in coalition, the price for which will be referendums on both the Euro and proportional representation.

By 2005, it will become apparent even to the Conservative Party, that Britain cannot remain outside the Single European Currency and still have much say in the future of Europe, for the future of Europe will be, by any other name, a United States of Europe, and, I suspect, in my lifetime.

The British: Reluctant Europeans was the sub-title of an article I published in 1989,[3] and it is the title of my Introduction. It hasn't changed much since then. The British are still the most reluctant of Europeans, save the Danes. This is a position of long standing. In a meeting in the Truman White House in 1949, British Foreign Secretary Ernest Bevin said 'Britain is too often accused of being the Bashful Boy in this sphere. Frankly, we do not consider ourselves a continental nation.'[4]

Polls and the Euro referendum

We measure five things with the tools of our trade: we can measure people's behaviour, what they do; we can measure their knowledge, what they know or think they know; and we can measure their views, and I break down views into three levels.

The first level is people's opinions, the 'ripples on the surface of the public consciousness,' easily blown about by the political winds and the media.

Below the surface are the currents of attitudes, which people have thought about, care about, have discussed with their families and friends, that impact on themselves and their families. Those attitudes are more strongly held and they are not easily blown about. You must have persuasion, you must have argument, and these must come from someone they respect and will listen to if they are to change.

Deeper still are the deep tides of the public's view which we call values - things like belief in God, the death penalty, euthanasia and, for 25 per cent of the British public, animal welfare. Other people's values focus on the environment, global warming and the like. Whatever it is that people feel deeply about, their values on these things change glacially, if at all.

Polls are not the same as referendums

Polls	Referendums
• Top of mind	• Considered
• Ongoing	• Day certain
• Not binding	• Morally binding
• Relatively unimportant	• Nationally important
• Not covered	• Media focus
• Wording vital	• Wording unimportant

Opinion polls are not the same as referendums. During the recent General Election the Leader of the Opposition tried to frighten the electorate with warnings that any referendum on the Euro would be 'rigged' as to timing and question wording. I consistently and continually hear from politicians: 'What matters is how you ask the question (and so forth) in a referendum.' They are wrong. Polls are top of mind. Referendums are not.

Polls are ongoing; here today, gone tomorrow. They are not binding. When an interviewer on behalf of a polling organisation asks you for your opinions, your attitudes or your values, your behaviour or your knowledge, it is not binding. You do not feel an obligation to think carefully and thoroughly about what it is that is being asked. It is relatively unimportant; it is not something you have thought about necessarily, you are just courteous enough to answer the questions. The media will not have covered the question matter in advance, for the most part, and the wording is vital.

Referenda on the other hand are considered. At the end of a three- or four-week campaign people know what is at issue, and the people who cast their vote have thought something about it. It is not sprung on them, nor is it a surprise to them that elicits an instant response. It is on a certain day; you know when it is. It is morally binding because you have been asked by your elected government to help them decide on an issue, normally of sovereignty, and this is why I am generally opposed to referendums. But in this instance, on the Euro, I believe everybody who has a vote - and I don't - should have the opportunity to have their say, because once sovereignty is given away it will never come back. Shared sovereignty is lost sovereignty in my view.

A referendum is by definition nationally important and because of that, it is the subject of media focus, and frankly the wording is very unimportant. Because of the wording of the Italian constitution, when they had a referendum on abortion, you had to vote 'No' to say 'Yes.' And so that was the slogan of the people who were for changing the constitution, because you had to vote no to say yes, and everybody knew exactly what was at issue and how they were voting. That is not so in an opinion poll.

The British: Reluctant Europeans

As the charts below show, 75 per cent of the British public say they feel strongly that they belong to the local community. 78 per cent said they feel strongly about England, or Scotland, or Wales - actually the Scots

Chart 1: How strongly do you feel you belong to the local community?

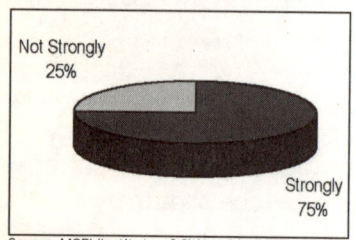

Source: MORI/Institute of Citizenship/NWB

Chart 2: How strongly do you feel you belong to England, Scotland, Wales?

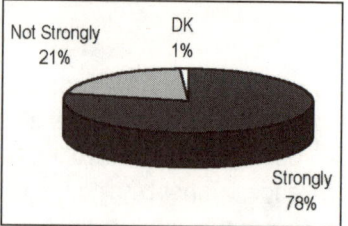

Source: MORI/Institute of Citizenship/NWB

Chart 3: How strongly do you feel you belong to Great Britain?

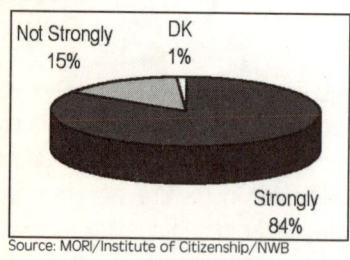

Source: MORI/Institute of Citizenship/NWB

Chart 4: How strongly do you feel you belong to Europe?

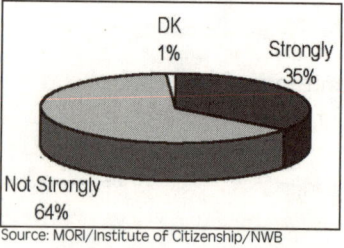

Source: MORI/Institute of Citizenship/NWB

and the Welsh were up in the 80 per cent range - and 84 per cent said they felt strongly that they belonged to Great Britain. But only 35 per cent said they felt strongly that they were Europeans.

In a survey we did a couple of years ago, only 29 per cent said they supported the Central Bank of Europe, whereas in Germany it was two-thirds. We know why, don't we? That is where the Central Bank of Europe was going to be sited. 45 per cent support and 40 per cent oppose fully

Chart 5: On balance, do you support or oppose a Central Bank of Europe?

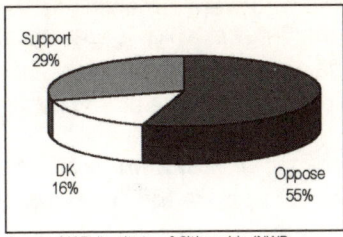

Source: MORI/Institute of Citizenship/NWB

Chart 6: On balance, do you support or oppose fully integrated armed forces?

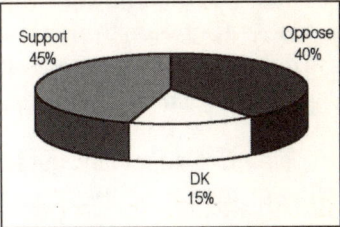

Source: MORI/Institute of Citizenship/NWB

Chart 7: On balance, do you support or oppose a single co-ordinated foreign policy?

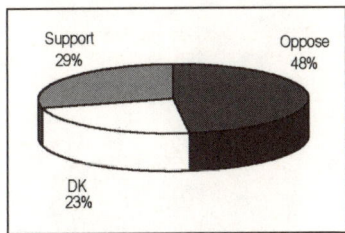

Source: MORI/Institute of Citizenship/NWB

Chart 8: On balance, do you support or opposed a United States of Europe with a Federal Government?

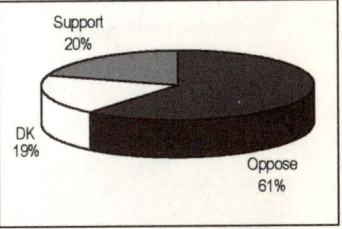

Source: MORI/Institute of Citizenship/NWB

integrated armed services, but nearly two to one (48 per cent to 29 per cent) oppose a single coordinated foreign policy, and only one in five said they supported a United States of Europe with a federal government.

Chart 9: Issues facing the country

Question: What are the most important issues facing the country?

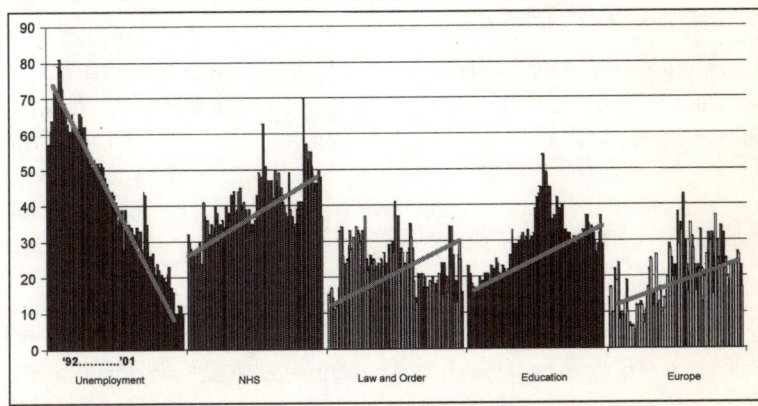

Source: MORI/The Times

The chart on the previous page shows that unemployment, which was the name of the game in the 1992 General Election, overwhelmingly, dropped to practically nothing in terms of public power, or public impact.

What has happened is that the unemployment response has been redistributed between the National Health Service, which is running high at the moment, law and order which is going up, education which is going up, and Europe which is going up, and they are all more or less parallel.

There is a more important question when it comes down to a General Election, or the run-up thereto, and that is: 'What are the issues that are important to you to determine how you are going to vote?' We find 65

Table 1: Issues that are important in deciding how to vote

1. Health Care	65%
2. Education	52%
3. Law and Order	47%
4. Taxation	31%
5. Europe	29%
6. Pensions	28%
7. Public Transport	27%
8. Managing the economy	27%

Source: MORI/The times
Base: 989 British Adults, 18+ 16-20 February 2001

per cent say healthcare is very important in helping decide which party to vote for; 52 per cent say education, and 47 per cent say law and order; and taxation - which is not even on the other chart - is in fourth place at 31 per cent, and Europe is at fifth place at 29 per cent.

Why issues don't 'bite'

There are four reasons why issues may fail to bite in determining how people vote in General Elections. First, they have to be salient. If you do not care about taxation, and it is thought not to be that important by 69 per cent of the British public, it isn't going to move you from one party to another. Secondly, you have to perceive differences between the parties on the issue. Thirdly, you must believe that the party would and, fourthly, could do something about it, if in power.

So where do the people who care about these issues stand? Which of the parties has the best policy among those who believe an issue to be important? This was the result in February of this year: healthcare, 44 per cent to 13 per cent Labour over the Tories; education, 46 per cent to 16 per cent Labour over the Tories. Law and order (where I've always expected the Tories to have a substantial lead) level pegging at 32 per cent to 32 per cent. Taxation, again a Tory issue in normal times, 30 per

Chart 10: Which party is best on the issues that are important in deciding how to vote (Based on those choosing)?

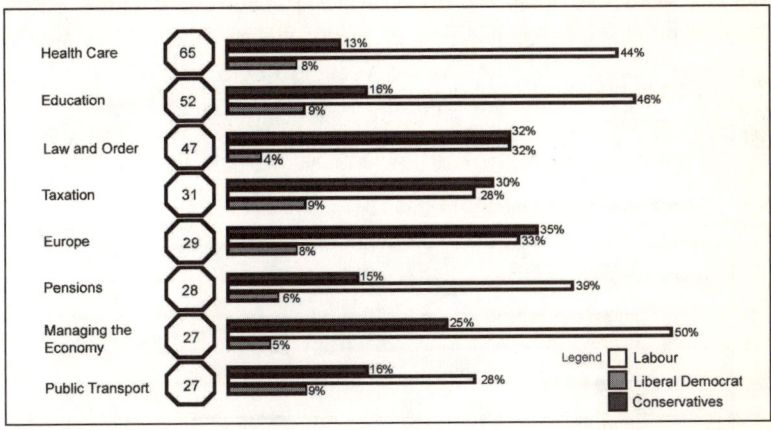

Source: MORI/The Times
989 British Adults 18+, 16-20 February 2001

cent to 28 per cent. Fascinatingly for this audience today, among the 29 per cent who say Europe is very important for them, 35 per cent to 33 per cent - level pegging; then pensions, managing the economy, public transport.

Unemployment and the environment, more or less level between Labour and the Liberal Democrats. Housing, four to one Labour. Only on defence

Chart 11: Which party is best on the issues that are important in deciding how to vote (Based on those choosing)?

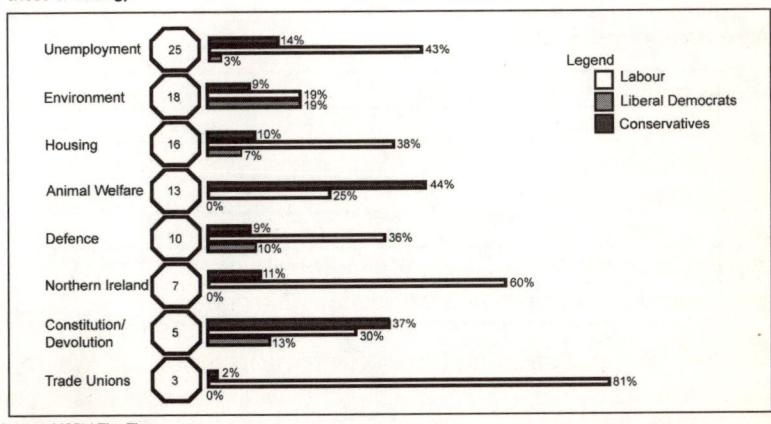

Source: MORI/ The Times
Base: 989 British Adults 18+, 16-20 February 2001

is there a substantial statistically significant lead for the Tory Party among the 13 per cent who give a fig about it anyway. Animal welfare nearly four to one Labour. Northern Ireland six to one Labour. Constitution/devolution, thought to be important by 5 per cent of the electorate, there you have a statistically significant 37 per cent to 30 per cent Tory lead.

In 1975, MORI was doing the polling for the Government's Referendum Campaign Group. Gallup had found that in January 1975, 55 per cent of the British public said they would vote to get out of the European Community and 45 per cent said they would vote to keep Britain in. They asked a very perceptive second question: 'If the government were to

Chart 12: The British: Reluctant Europeans

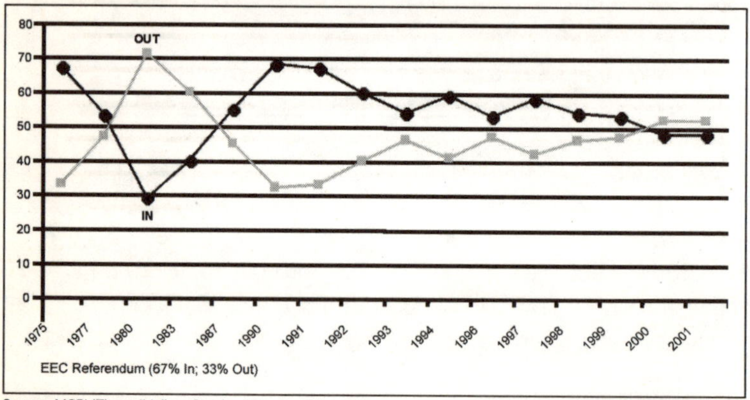

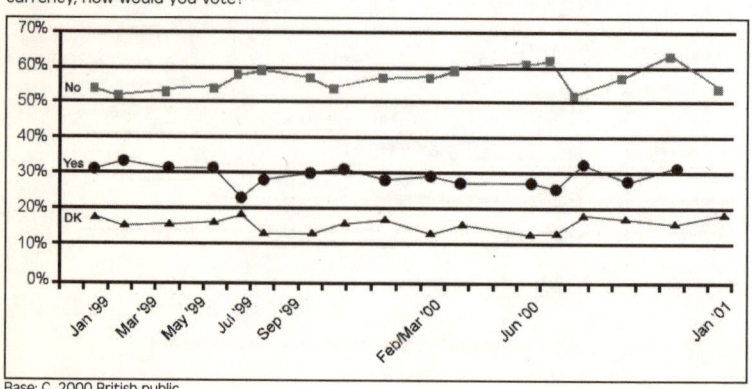

Source: MORI/Times/Mail on Sunday/ Sunday Telegraph
Base: c. 2000 British

Chart 13: Single European Currency
Question: If there were a referendum now on whether Britain should be part of a single European currency, how would you vote?

Base: C, 2000 British public
Source: MORI/Schroder Salomon Smith Barney

renegotiate the terms and strongly urge that Britain stay in, then how would you vote?' And it came up with 69 per cent to 31 per cent to stay in - and the result, as shown on the left-hand side of chart 12, was 67 per cent to 33 per cent - very well predicted.

So, if there were a referendum now on whether Britain should be part of a single European currency, how would you vote?

Chart 14: Single European Currency
Question: If there were a referendum now on whether Britain should be part of a single European currency, how would you vote (excluding 'don't knows')?

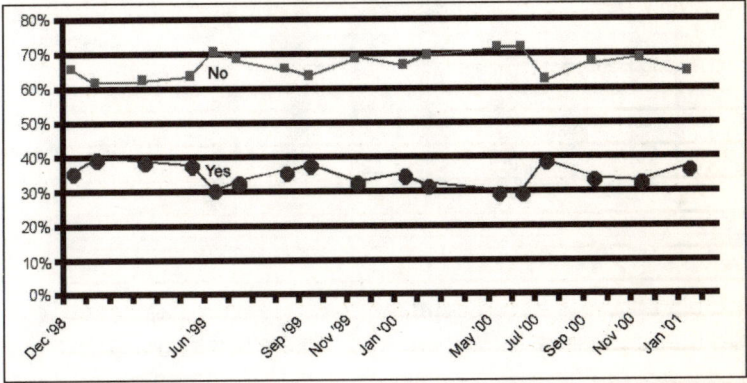

Base: C, 2000 British public
Source: MORI/Schroder Salomon Smith Barney

Chart 15: Single European Currency
Question A: If there were a referendum now on whether Britain should be part of a single European currency, how would you vote (excluding 'don't knows')?
Question B. 'If the goverment were to strongly urge that Britain should be part of the single currency how would you vote

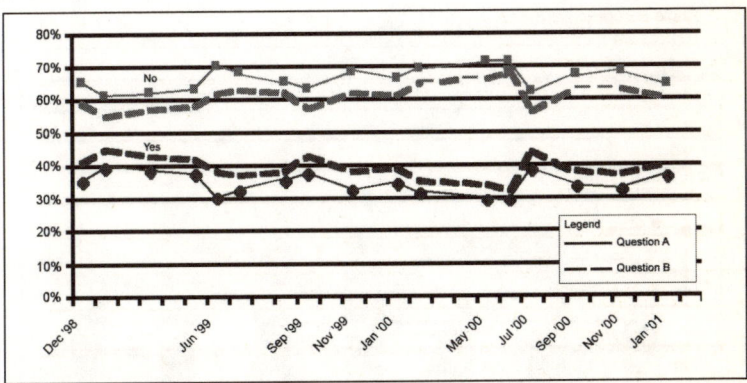

Base: c, 2000 British public
Source: MORI/Schroeder Salomon Smith Barney

This is a question we ask every two months. It makes about a five-point swing to the difference, so it narrows it a bit, but nothing like so much as it did in 1975.

Chart 16: Single European Currency
Question: Which of the following best describes you own view of British participation in the single currency?

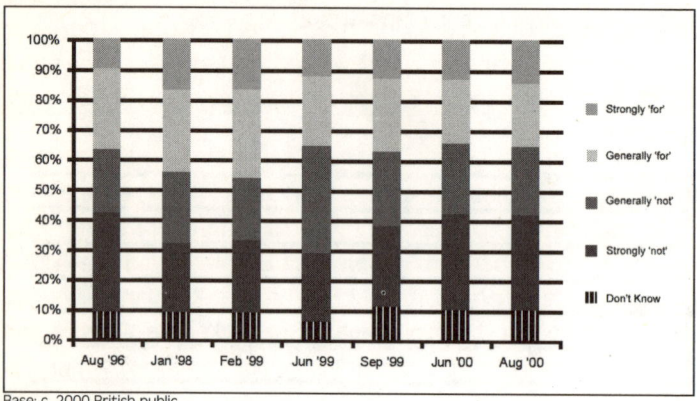

Base: c, 2000 British public
Source: MORI/The Times/ Sunday Telegraph/TGWU

But I do not think that is a sufficiently sensitive question. I have been able to ask half a dozen times, as shown here: 'Which of the following best describes your own view of British participation in the single European currency?'

The group I focus on are not the people whose values are whether Britain is in or out, but the people whose attitudes and opinions are in the middle group, because the middle group is the group that can be swung.

Chart 17: Single European Currency
Question: Which of the following best describes you own view of British participation in the single currency?

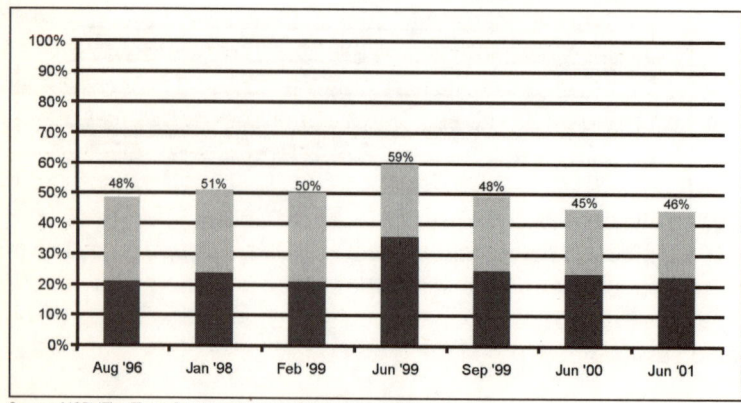

Source: MORI/The Times Sunday Telegraph/TGWU/GrahamBishop.com
Base: c. 2000 British public

If I take just those, these are the percentages that will be the battleground of the Euro referendum, which is about political consent and not economic convergence. This is for the hearts and minds of a very substantial number of people. In July of 2000, when I published the booklet for the Foreign Policy Centre drawing on my experience in 1975, I was able to say: 'It is possible - just - to swing 22 per cent of the British public on this issue, if it is a parallel to the 1975 experience.' From January 1975, when it was 55 per cent to 45 per cent to get out, to the result in June 1975 of 67 per cent to 33 per cent to stay in, is a swing of 22 points.

If at the time I wrote that - which was May/June 2000 - I took the polls I was doing and projected those and applied a 22 per cent swing, it came out 52 per cent to 48 per cent in favour of Britain joining the Euro. My conclusion was the referendum could be held in October or November of 2001 in the honeymoon following a British General Election which would be won, handily, by the Labour Party, (which it was) on June 7.

In 1975 however you had all the parties saying, 'Vote in.' You had most or all of the newspapers except *The Tribune* saying, 'Vote in.' You had virtually all the top businessmen, the captains of industry, saying, 'Vote in.' You had the trade union barons saying, 'Vote in,' and 'Vote out' was being said by 'the men with staring eyes' as they were called at the time.

So, what are we looking at today: at the recent election, another landslide, therefore no power by the Lib Dems this time either to force a referendum on the Euro. A very short honeymoon. The introduction of the Single European Currency and coinage on 1 January 2002 and chaos for six months - by the end of which, in my view, there will be mid-term blues, and it would not be a referendum on the Euro in 2003, as it would be a referendum on the standing of the Government, the way it was in France when they voted on Maastricht. That is why I do not think there will be a referendum on the Euro in the life of the next parliament.

What's more, the British public agree with me. In a recent survey[5] carried out for GrahamBishop.Com, a majority, 52 per cent, of the British public said that whatever their personal view of membership, they thought it was likely that people in Britain will regularly use a single European currency and coinage in 2005 (34 per cent thought not), and three people in four, 74 per cent, said they thought it was likely by 2010.

Notes

[1] Professor Robert M. Worcester, Chairman, MORI, 32 Old Queen St., London SW1 9HP, Tel. 020-7222-0232, Fax. 020-7227-0404, email: worc@mori.com, web site: www.mori.com

[2] Worcester, R., *How to Win the Euro Referendum: Lessons from 1975*, London: The Foreign Policy Centre, July 2000.

[3] Worcester, R., 'European Attitudes to the EC,' *European Business Journal*, Volume 1, Issue 4, 1989, pp.33-42.

[4] White House Memorandum of Conversation of Private Meeting 3 April 1949.

[5] MORI Research Study, 'Joining the Euro,' for Granam Bishop.com, 1,983 British adults 15+, 14-19 June 2001 carried out face-to-face in respondents' homes in 187 sampling points throughout Great Britain.

Chapter 2

Winning the Euro Argument

by David Clark

Editor's Commentary

Bob Worcester may be right in his prognosis, but we do not yet know, and many (on both sides of the argument) believe there is still all to fight for. He is certainly right to suggest there is a first argument still to win: whether to hold the referendum (and not just examine the five tests) before the end of 2003. In a sense in response, **David Clark**, *with four years' experience inside the Foreign Office, underlines what the Government needs to do to open up the debate and help to 'Persuade the People.'*

Winning the Euro Argument

by David Clark

Against all odds?

The first obstacle that will have to be overcome if Britain is to join the Euro is that the Government will need to feel confident that a referendum is winnable. Although the formal position is that the Chancellor's five economic tests are the only barrier to membership, it is clear that the Government will not call a referendum unless it feels there is a reasonable prospect of success.

On the surface of it, the available evidence is discouraging, with opinion polls persistently showing majorities of around two to one against. But Government strategists have always had a more nuanced view of public opinion, believing that opposition to the Euro is wide, but shallow. In other words, they believe that many of those who say they are currently opposed are in practice are 'soft sceptics' who could be persuaded to vote 'yes' in a referendum if they felt that Britain would benefit by joining. The model often cited is the 1975 referendum on EEC membership in which a 55 per cent to 45 per cent margin in favour of withdrawal was turned into a 67 per cent to 33 per cent vote for staying in within the space of sixth months.

There is plenty of evidence to support this thesis. Surveys regularly indicate that a sizeable proportion of those who say they would vote against entry if there were a referendum today also say they could be persuaded to change their minds. An opinion poll conducted by MORI shortly after the General Election produced the following result: 13 per cent strongly support British participation; 23 per cent are generally in favour, but could vote against if they thought it would be bad for the British economy; 24 per cent are generally opposed, but could vote in favour if they thought it would be good for the British economy; and 31 per cent are strongly opposed. With only 44 per cent of the electorate strongly committed one way or the other, there is evidently a lot to play for. Further evidence of the softness and volatility of public opinion can be found in various experiments that have been conducted to test the arguments on sample groups of electors, most recently in the BBC's *Referendum Street* documentary. Here, exposure to the arguments in a mock referendum turned a clear majority against entry into a clear majority in favour.

Another indicator is the large majority who consistently say that membership of the Euro is inevitable. Political strategists who want to get an accurate picture of what the public really thinks will often look at polling data on what they expect to happen. In the 1992 General Election, for example, most opinion polls put Labour ahead when respondents were asked how they intended to vote. The same opinion polls, however, also showed that most voters expect the Conservatives to win, which they did.

MORI's post-election poll showed that the timeframe within which the British people expect to be using Euro notes and coins had shortened, with 52 per cent expecting them to be in circulation by 2005 and 34 per cent believing that sterling will still be in use. This reversed MORI's findings of sixth months earlier, which produced a margin of 50 per cent to 41 per cent in favour of those who think sterling will still be in use by 2005. Clearly the electorate both expect the Government to hold a referendum in this parliament and to be persuaded to vote in favour of entry.

1975 and all that

On the basis of the available evidence, the Government has every reason to conclude that a Euro referendum is winnable in the right conditions. But there are several crucial flaws in its assumptions about how this can be done. Over-reliance on 1975 as a precedent is one of them. The Prime Minister's communications chief, Alistair Campbell, is known to believe that an intensive sixth month campaign could, once again, prove sufficient to turn public opinion around. This ignores the point that the differences between 1975 and today are, in most respects, greater than the similarities. For a start, a 'yes' vote in 1975 was a vote for the status quo. Britain had already been in the EEC for two and a half years, which meant that the innate conservatism of the British electorate favoured the pro-European argument. In a future Euro referendum, the

Government will be faced with the inherently more difficult task of persuading the electorate to take a voyage into the unknown.

Another important difference lies in the nature of the forces that will line up on either side. In 1975 there was an overwhelming consensus of elite opinion on the pro-European side. The leaderships of the three major parties, virtually every major business, most trade union leaders and almost all national newspapers campaigned for a 'yes' vote. Even *The Sun* was in favour. A referendum on the Euro will produce a much more divided picture. The Conservative Party will remain firmly opposed for the foreseeable future. Thanks largely to *The Sun* and *The Daily Mail*, they will be joined by the overwhelming preponderance of newspapers weighted according to readership. Although businesses will be mostly in favour, a substantial number are likely to remain ambivalent, with only exporters seeing a very strong interest in joining.

In seeking a mandate for Euro entry, pro-Europeans face a much greater challenge in the face of much stronger opposition than they did in 1975. Dealing with this ought to have major implications for the timing and duration of a campaign. An intensive six-month burst may not be enough to turn public opinion around unless external events intervene to radically alter British perceptions of the Euro's performance. The latest Eurobarometer survey, which indicated very low levels of public knowledge of the issues, suggests that a much longer period of up to a full year may be needed to prepare the ground for a successful referendum.

The Government will also need to understand that the longer the referendum is left, the harder it will become. Mid-term referendums are notoriously tricky, even with an establishment consensus in support. The Danish and Irish governments have both lost European referendums in the last year, a fate President Mitterrand only narrowly avoided over Maastricht in 1992. Tony Blair will face much stronger opposition than they did, so he would be well advised to separate the issue from any consideration of mid-term popularity. These factors mean that a referendum needs to be held before the end of 2002, with the campaign to persuade the British people starting a year earlier.

It's the Euro, stupid

Another flaw in the Government's approach has been to treat the issue of the Euro as separable from the wider question of Britain's engagement in Europe. Alarmed by the sharp increase in support for withdrawal from the European Union since the early 1990s, the strategy of the Government in the last parliament was to focus on building stronger and wider support for Britain's EU membership. This was seen as a prerequisite for the launch of a campaign in favour of the single currency. The cross-party Britain in Europe campaign was launched in 1999 with an instruction to ignore the Euro and go back to first principles. But this 'don't mention the Euro' approach failed to halt the decline in public support for either the Euro or the European Union. To their credit, Britain in Europe have recognised the futility of the strategy originally imposed on them and started to make some of the arguments in favour of joining the Euro. But they will fail to make much headway unless the Government is prepared to follow suit.

The Government's refusal to open up debate on the Euro arises from a basic misunderstanding of public opinion. Although voters regularly complain of a lack of information about Economic and Monetary Union, they intuitively understand that the decision on whether or not to join the Euro is inextricably linked to the question of Britain's position in the EU. Eurobarometer's graph tracking public opinion over the last twenty years illustrates this point quite clearly. It shows support for the EU membership peaking at the height of the Single Market programme in 1990, going into steep decline during the negotiation of the Maastricht Treaty in 1991 and continuing to decline gradually throughout the 1990s. Although the end of the Cold War may have had some effect in reducing the perceived need for European integration, there can be no doubt that the fears and anxieties created by the debate about Economic and Monetary Union have been the most significant factor in reducing support for the European Union itself.

By seeking to concentrate on the issue of 'Europe in or out,' while ignoring the Euro, the Government has been guilty of treating the symptoms and not the cause of Britain's eurosceptic malady. If Tony Blair wants to get Britain into to the Euro, he will need to give up the illusion that he can win the debate by proxy and start to engage on the central issue at stake. The British people will never be at ease with the European Union until they are persuaded that Economic and Monetary Union is a logical and desirable part of its development, rather than a threatening and unnecessary imposition.

The national economic interest

In framing the arguments that will persuade the British people to back entry, the most hotly debated issue is whether the Euro is a political or an economic question. The view of the Government is quite clear: the decision on Euro entry should be taken on the basis of Britain's national economic interests alone. There is, as the Prime Minister has repeatedly said, 'no constitutional bar' to membership and it only remains for the Chancellor's five economic tests to be met before Britain can join.

There is certainly no shortage of economic arguments in favour of membership. Provided it follows policies of macroeconomic stability, a larger currency zone will be able to maintain lower interest rates across the economic cycle, leading to lower borrowing costs for businesses and homeowners alike. The elimination of exchange rate risk will remove the need for British exporters to hedge against currency fluctuations that often disrupt trade with their main markets inside the eurozone. This will remove a significant cost burden, which can be prohibitively high for small and medium-sized enterprises in particular, along with a source of instability that can wipe out profit margins overnight. Absolute price transparency across a market of 360 million people will empower consumers and businesses to seek the cheapest supply source, increasing competition and exerting downward pressure on prices. Many of these benefits can be presented in terms that will be easily recognisable to British voters, such as lower mortgages, greater stability and an end to 'rip-off Britain.'

As well as engaging in the argument about bread and butter issues, the pro-Euro campaign will also need to project some of the strategic economic arguments in favour of Economic and Monetary Union. This will require a major exercise in explaining the role that currencies play in modern economic life. At a very basic level, this will involve tackling popular misconceptions about the terms 'weak' and 'strong' as they apply to exchange rates. More fundamentally, there is an argument to be made about the effect that currency barriers have in restricting trade and retarding economic development.

Professor Andrew Rose of the University of California has analysed the historical data comparing trade patterns within and between currency zones. His conclusion is that economies sharing the same currency trade approximately three times more than economies that don't. Put simply, the larger the currency zone, the greater the volume of trade. With that additional trade comes huge economies of scale and more choice, leading to lower prices and higher productivity levels as companies absorb efficiency savings and start to feel the pressure of more intense competition. It is this, and not simply differences in labour market flexibility, that explains the divergence of American and European economic performance over the last two decades. The Americans enjoy a huge economic advantage that we have denied ourselves by maintaining separate European currencies.

Establishing this thought in the minds of the British electorate will have two positive consequences. First, by breaking the psychological link between national strength and monetary sovereignty, it can form the basis of a strong patriotic argument for why Britain should join the Euro. Keeping the pound is not a means of guaranteeing our economic strength, but of perpetuating our economic weakness relative to America. Second, it will help to transfer the burden of risk from 'pros' to the 'antis.' The rest of Europe is forging ahead without us. Unfettered by exchange rates barriers, our European partners will achieve an efficiency and intensity of economic activity dwarfing everything that has so far been achieved and turning the eurozone into the real Single Market. Outside, Britain will suffer a gradual loss of competitiveness as British companies remain locked in behind currency barriers and a reduction in inward investment as foreign companies seek to eliminate currency risk by locating inside the eurozone.

The importance of politics

The economic arguments for the Euro are compelling, but pro-Europeans will fatally weaken their case if they fail to engage in the political and constitutional issues involved. The Government's insistence that it is simply a question of economics and that the constitutional issues have been 'settled' is patronising and will prove unconvincing to an electorate for whom the constitutional arguments are far from settled. Earlier this year Eurobarometer found that 63 per cent of those surveyed agreed with the proposition that giving up the pound would mean an end to national independence. If that figure remains the same, it is difficult to see how a referendum can be won.

There is a huge task here for pro-Europeans to explain the relationship between the political and economic dimensions of the European Union, one that has been delayed for far too long. There is an abiding myth that Britain was tricked in 1975 into voting for a free trade area that subsequently became a political union. There was no such deception, but the narrow focus of the 'yes' campaign on the economic arguments meant that they missed an opportunity to resolve this issue once and for all. In a Euro referendum, the 'no' campaign will argue that pro-Europeans are trying to pull the same 'trick' again. It is an argument that is likely to strike a chord with the electorate unless the 'yes' campaign is able to argue confidently and pro-actively on the political merits of their case.

A key objective must be to demolish the futile argument about whether the European Union is a political or and economic project. It is both, and necessarily so, because the politics and economics of European integration are indivisible. The objectives of the founding fathers (European unity and an end to war) were certainly political. But the means by which they could be delivered were economic; the closest integration of economic interests through creation of a common (later single) market. Since markets can only operate fairly and effectively within the rule of law, it logically follows that a common/single market requires a strong legal framework, efficient political bodies to frame its laws and a court with binding authority to adjudicate where there are disputes. In other words, economic union requires a degree of political union and vice versa. There is nothing more perverse in British politics that the claim of some eurosceptics to love the Single Market, but hate all the things that have made it possible.

The same logic applies to Economic and Monetary Union. If we want the economic benefits of being part of a larger currency zone, we have to accept the inevitable political consequences in the form monetary decision-making by an independent European Central Bank and the restrictions on budget deficits contained in the Stability Pact. These should be accepted enthusiastically, not reluctantly, because the gains are real, while the sacrifices are only apparent. Global markets already impose heavy constraints on what national governments can do. That is the reason why Britain concluded that national political control of monetary policy was more of a hindrance than a help when the Bank of England was made independent. The loss of sovereignty involved in transferring that power to the ECB is purely theoretical. The deficit limits in the Stability Pact are, in practice, no greater than those any sensible government would accept if it wished to maintain economic stability and market confidence. Indeed, the extra growth generated from participation in the Euro will reduce rather than increase pressures on public spending.

Our political strength will be enhanced, rather than weakened, through the process of pooling monetary sovereignty. We will be part of a larger currency bloc that is in the process of becoming a global counterpart to the dollar. Enhanced economic strength will bring greater political clout and the opportunity to play a pivotal role in a Europe that punches its weight in the world. And we will have a place in the key decision-making bodies that affect the performance the Single Market of which we are an integral part. Outside the eurozone, we face gradual political marginalisation as the artificial distinction between the Euro-related issues and the rest of the EU policy field breaks down and the fact of Economic and Monetary Union exerts an ever-greater pull on more and more spheres of decision-making. As with the economic case, the political risk lies in not joining.

Conclusion

The referendum can be won. The message of the opinion polls is that the British people sense that there is an inescapable logic that will eventually lead Britain to join the Euro, even if their political leaders are failing to explain it to them. But against a backdrop of more than a decade in which successive governments have tried to push the issue of British membership of the Euro under the carpet, the argument will not be won quickly or easily. It will require an intensive campaign in which the Government is prepared to give a strong lead by setting out a vision of Britain's future in which our wholehearted participation in the European Union, including the Euro, is an indispensable element.

Chapter 3

Lessons of the 1975 Referendum

by Ernest Wistrich

Editor's Commentary

Before looking in more detail at the arguments for and against joining the single European currency, it is useful to remind ourselves of the experience of the 1975 referendum on continued British membership of the European Community, as it then was. **Ernest Wistrich**, *as Director of the European Movement, master-minded the successful campaign for Britain to remain a member. As he points out, although the forthcoming referendum will have a less general focus, in fact the fundamental questions are very similar: the economic costs and benefits, and the political arguments around the question of national sovereignty. This time the latter are likely to have more emphasis – and in my view rightly so.*

Although opinion in 2001 still shows a majority against sterling joining the Euro, the article points to the volatility of British public opinion on the subject of Europe. Following Bob Worcester's arguments, the first key question will be the role and then impact of the Government, which before the June election (or even immediately afterwards) was not exactly zealous in promoting the principle of early membership. Many contributors are convinced it must play an early and much more active role in proselytising the cause if opinion is to be swung round. Unlike 1975, when the media were largely in favour of continuing membership of the European Community, those now in favour of joining the Euro have to contend with a largely hostile press, and an opposition with much greater financial resources than last time. Ernest Wistrich nevertheless argues that the referendum can be won by those in favour.

Lessons of the 1975 Referendum

by Ernest Wistrich

Following the return of a Labour government to power in 2001 a referendum on whether to adopt the single currency is likely to be held during its second term of office. This will be the second national referendum on Europe, the first having been held in 1975 to confirm continued British membership of the European Community (the predecessor of the European Union). That referendum took place following the regeneration by the Labour government of the terms of membership on which Britain entered in 1973. Although the issues to be considered are different this time the same broad topics will be debated: the economic costs and benefits and political arguments about the loss of national sovereignty.

The purpose of this chapter is to look at the issues before both referendums, at public attitudes now and then, and see whether lessons can be drawn from our experiences of the 1970s, which could assist the pro-Europeans in the conduct of the campaign preceding the referendum on the Euro.

Public opinion on membership

From the Eurobarometer survey of Public attitudes, conducted for the European Commission in July 2001, it appears that support in Britain for the European Union is near to its lowest level since we joined the EEC in 1973. Only some 29 per cent believed that EU membership was a good thing for our country. 24 per cent thought it was bad for us, with 27 per cent thinking that it was neither good nor bad leaving some 20 per cent who did not know. Support for the Euro dropped 36 per cent in the autumn of 1998 to 28 per cent in 1999 and then fell to only 22 per cent by 2000. Since than it has risen slightly to 25 per cent. However, a large majority of those questioned said that they did not know enough about the issues to make up their minds and wishing to be better informed. Last year's Eurobarometer asked people to rate their knowledge of the EU out of 10, where 10 means 'know a great deal,' 1 means 'know nothing a all.' The British gave themselves 3.78 out of 10.

If we look at public opinion during the period preceding our entry into the EEC and before the referendum on staying in, we find that British attitudes on joining the European Community were highly favourable when the Conservative government under Harold Macmillan applied for membership in 1961. Nearly 50 per cent approved with less than 20 per cent against joining, and the rest did not know. After the first veto against our membership by the French president Charles de Gaulle in 1963, enthusiasm for membership declined somewhat, but then rose quite dramatically when the Labour Government under Harold Wilson applied again in 1976. 70 per cent were in favour with less than 10 per cent against. The House of Commons, after a weeklong debate in May 1967 voted in favour of a second application to join by an unprecedented 85 per cent of its membership of all political parties. However, when do Gaulle vetoed British entry for the second time at the end of 1967, public opinion changed dramatically. Nearly 50 per cent became opposed a membership with those in favour dropping down to about 35 per cent. Favourable attitudes declined even further, in spite of de Gaulle's resignation in 1969 and a new opportunity being offered to negotiate entry once again. In preparing for the negotiations, the Labour government produced a White paper in the spring of 1970 to set out the costs and benefits of membership. The costs, largely related to food price increases likely to follow British acceptance of the Community's Common Agricultural Policy, were clearly spelt out. The benefits on the other way hand, whilst described in general terms, were not quantified. Public reaction to the White Paper was dramatic with support for membership plummeting even further. By December 1970, when negotiations for entry by the new Conservative government were in full wing, 70 per cent of the public declared themselves against membership with only some 18 per cent in favour. During 1971 support improved and by the time the negotiations were successfully concluded the public once again moved in favour with a small majority of 45 per cent against 41 per cent.

Britain entered the EEC in 1973. At the end of the year the war in the Middle East precipitated a world economic crisis following the quadrupling of oil prices and similar massive increases in other raw materials. Soon these affected all price levels. Many in Britain identified the price increases as a direct result of our entry into the EEC. By 1974 opinion turned against EEC membership once again with some 40 per cent wanting to leave the Community and only 24 per cent in favour of continues membership.

These polls illustrate the volatility of public opinion on European Community membership which, certainly up to then, had had little direct effect of the lives of British citizens, their uncertainty about the issue and a string desire for more guidance. Indeed it was significant that, when Edward Heath's Conservative government and Harold Wilson's Labour administration concluded their respective negotiations and recommended acceptance of the terms, public opposition declined and support for membership overtook those against. In 1975 the change in public attitudes was quite dramatic. Once the renegotiations for new terms of membership had been concluded and the government recommended their acceptance in April 1975, public opinion followed suit and moved to a 2 to 1 majority in favour.

Issues debated

Turning to the issues which now dominate the debate on the Euro, the economic arguments about the adoption of the single currency concentrate on the risks and potential benefits. The risks deal with the probable costs of conversion, and the problems associated with a single monetary policy for the whole of the eurozone where member states have different inflation rates, asymmetrical economic cycles and structural difference. Against these, the arguments in favour are about monetary stability and the consequential retention and attraction of foreign investment, the further growth of trade leading to higher living standards and direct benefits to consumers following the adoption of the lower interest rates ruling within the eurozone. These economic arguments are not easy for the general public to follow. The debate is increasingly shifting to associated political issues concerned with the abandonment of our own currency, which is portrayed as a symbol of our national identity, and the potential loss of national sovereignty in managing our own economy. The opponents of the Euro extend their arguments by claiming that Economic and Monetary Union with a single currency is merely a stepping stone to the creation as a centralised European super-state of which they want no part. There is growing opposition to any further steps of EU integration and a demand to renegotiate Britain's whole relationship with the EU, which would logically lead to ultimate withdrawal.

The debates concerned with membership of the EEC in the 1970s similarly included arguments about the economic costs and benefits. The costs were largely related to rises in food prices as a result of the Common Agriculture Policy. The benefits were seen as a result of joining an economically fast growing Community, most of whose members had overtaken British living standards over the period since its formation. Although the arguments about the loss of political independence played a role, the potential rise in the cost of living dominated the debates. Arguments about the loss of national sovereignty were much less used and less significant the 1970s than they are now.

Role of campaigns

As indicated above, the attitudes of governments to the issues being submitted for decision in a referendum can sway the public substantially. But referendums conducted on European issues by our EU partners did not always result in decisions recommended by their Governments. Several referendums in Norway and Denmark went against their Governments' advice and the French referendum, on the Maastricht Treaty, was approved by a minuscule majority. Furthermore politicians in Britain no longer command the same trust and respect amongst the electorate as they did in the past and the public are less likely to be swayed by their arguments. In consequence the nature of the campaigns conducted ahead of referenda can play an important role in influencing the results.

In approaching the next referendum we need also to look at the role of the media. The attitude of the press has changed since the 1970s. In those days there was almost universal press support for British entry into the EEC, with only the *Daily Express* and the Communist *Morning Star* arguing against. Now the position has changed. The majority of newspapers, especially those owned by Rupert Murdoch and Conrad Black, have consistently opposed both the Euro and any further European integration, and proposals by the European Commission are always castigated. The hostile papers include *The Times*, *The Daily Telegraph*, *The Daily Mail*, *The Sun* and their Sunday titles. The opinion of the remaining papers is more balanced and a number are good supporters of the Euro and further European integration. By law broadcasting has to display an even handed treatment of the issues and both radio and television have largely followed the rules. In the 1970s, while retaining their neutrality, both radio and TV were instrumental in widely informing the public about life and politics in the EEC countries. This played an important role in lessening anti-European prejudice. Much will depend on a similar role played by the broadcasters once the referendum on the Euro is announced. Equally important will be the role of multiple Channel Television and the ever-increasing use of web sites.

The campaign for EEC entry 1970/1

If any lessons are to be learnt about the campaign of the 1970s it will be relevant to cover, not jut the 1974/5 referendum period, but also the campaign preceding entry as they both dealt with the same issue, namely Britain's membership of the EEC.

When the Conservatives came to power in June 1970, the government took over the negotiating strategy prepared by the preceding Labour administration. Edward Heath, the Prime Minister, was a long-term supporter of British participation in European integration, so the attempt to join was given maximum priority. The government did, however, face a dilemma. Negotiations promised to be complex and tough. The government could not fight vigorously for British interests and, at the same time, laud uncritically the benefits of membership.

So Geoffrey Rippon, the minister in charge of the negotiations, asked the European Movement to undertake the task of persuading the public in favour of entry. Although the final decision was left to parliament, MPs were unlikely to approve entry against a very hostile electorate. As already indicted above, at the end of 1970 support for entry had dropped to some 18 per cent with a massive 70 per cent opposed.

The European Movement accepted the challenge of organising the campaign. The first was to set out solid and convincing arguments in favour and ensuring their widest dissemination. Some two hundred voluntary lecturers were recruited and public meetings were organised. Every conceivable type of local organisation was encouraged to hold meetings for their members, at which the Movement's speakers would explain the issues. During the first six months of 1971 over one thousand of such meetings were held throughout the country. Some included debates with opponents, but most consisted of speakers setting out the reasons for and benefits of EEC membership. Large numbers of leaflets were produced and the Movement started publishing a popular monthly eight-page newspaper called 'The British European.' Some leaflets pointed to the loss in earnings suffered by the British because they were not part if the economically faster growing community, and others made comparisons of living standards, social security benefits and taxation. The newspaper was designed for a popular readership with cartoons and many photographs illustrating the benefits of EEC membership. Volunteers, including girls wearing tee shirts with the slogan 'Europe or Bust' distributed over 10 million copies of the leaflets and the newspaper freely throughout the country. The campaign in the country was organised by paid regional organisers employed by the Movement. A major advertising campaign was carried out in the national press over several months. One highly successful advert illustrated a schoolboy with a text below of 'Give him cheap butter now and let him worry about where his bread is coming from later.' Several hundred large wall posters were displayed on billboards with a photograph of a group of children waving the flags of both EEC members and candidate countries, with a large slogan 'Say Yes to Europe.' Articles and letters were prepared and organised to appear in the national, regional and local press, often written by prominent personalities with varied backgrounds and occupations. A pop record was produced recording a song with the refrain 'We've got to get in to get on.' It was played at meetings and gained some popularity by being broadcast on the radio several times. The same slogan was used on window bills and car stickers.

The campaign lasted some six months and cost around one million pounds. The funds were raised largely from business, and no funds were provided by the Government. At the end of the campaign, when negotiations for entry were concluded, public opinion swung towards a small majority in favour. As a result, parliamentarians, who has the task of approving the agreement reached, were not inhibited by previous public hostility in arriving at their decision.

The referendum campaign 1974/5

The Labour Party did not reject British membership of the EEC but objected to the terms negotiated for entry by the Conservative government. To avoid a split in between Labour pro and anti-Europeans, the party had made a commitment that once returned to power, it would renegotiate the terms of membership and if successful, submit the results to a national referendum allowing party members freedom to campaign on both sides of the argument. When Labour was returned to office in 1974 a referendum was clearly on the cards. This was to be the first national referendum in British constitutional history, without precedent or experience to guide its conduct.

Once again the European Movement started to plan for the forthcoming campaign. An in-depth survey of opinion was conducted in June 1974 to determine the state of public opinion on the issue. The results of survey showed a two to one majority against membership. The survey also set out to discover the reasons of those questioned for their attitudes and their reaction to various arguments advanced during the interview.

Because Britain lacked experience of referendums, it was decided to investigate the conduct of the campaigns on EEC membership organised in 1972 in Ireland, Denmark and Norway. In the first two countries substantial majorities were obtained in favour of membership. In Norway the opposition won the campaign and the country did not join the EEC. All the campaigns provided valuable data and techniques, which could also be applied in Britain. Most remarkable, however, was the campaign by the opponents of membership in Norway. Faced with almost unanimous support for entry by the establishment, including the government, the largest political parties, business, trade unions and the media, the opposition had developed a distinctive campaign. This avoided the unanimity of the pro-Europeans and all of them speaking with one voice on the subject. Opponents of entry represented a whole variety of interests, each putting forward their own reasons for opposing EEC membership. Thus Norwegian fishermen campaigned to preserve their territorial waters and traditional fishing rights. Protestants warned against the dangers posed by Rome and the dominant role of the Catholics in the EEC. Every town formed a local representative group of citizens who argued the disadvantages of EEC membership for their localities. The multiplicity of different arguments against overcame the solid and unanimous front of the establishment and those in favour of Norwegian entry were defeated in the referendum.

Reports on the experience of the referendum in Ireland, Denmark and Norway provided valuable guidance on the conduct of the British referendum campaign. It was agreed to adopt a strategy largely based on the Norwegian anti EEC campaign. However, the European Movement had a problem vis-à-vis the British electorate. After its wide-ranging, vigorous and highly partisan campaign in favour of entry in 1971 it was seen as a movement of federalist Euro-fanatics with excessively partisan views. A number of favourably inclined organisations in the country would therefore have found it difficult to co-operate with the Movement. To overcome this handicap it was agreed to create a new organisation called 'Britain in Europe' and suspend the activities of the European Movement for a period of six months before the referendum. All Movement staff, members and supporters were to act under the common 'Britain in Europe' umbrella.

After the second General Election in the autumn of 1974, which was won by Labour with an increased majority, negotiations for changing the terms of membership were started. Legislation was introduced to hold the referendum after this was completed. The 6 June 1975 was designated as the referendum date. In the legislation two official organisations were recognised as the protagonists of the 'Yes' and 'No' votes and each was allocated a government grant of £125,000. They were allowed to raise their own funds from private sources, but once the official campaign started, the names of all donors above £1000 had to be declared.

Britain in Europe, leading the 'Yes' campaign, received endorsement form business, the trade unions, academic and from well known politicians. The campaign was put into high gear at the beginning of 1975 and its slogan 'Keep Britain in Europe' received the widest publicity.

To build up an active army of supporters the European Movement had, already in the autumn of 1974, distributed a leaflet to nearly every household in the UK. Entitled 'Out of Europe – Out of work' it appealed for volunteers to help in the forthcoming campaign. A distribution of some 6.5 million leaflets yielded about 12,000 volunteers. Seventeen regional organisers were employed with the task of organising the helpers into appropriate groups and give them guidance. Some 600 speakers were trained and they addressed several thousand meetings.

In every town, committees were formed such as 'Brighton in Europe,' 'Oxford in Europe' etc. Each committee had a non-party chair but included representatives of all the major political parties. Co-operation between them was often a novel experience, but was generally highly successful. Every local society and non-governmental organisation favourably inclined was invited to take an active part. The committees' principle role was to work out the reasons why their locality would benefit from membership of the EEC and then to publicise them. They recruited further supported, distributed leaflets supplied from the centre, organised meetings, conducted local press campaigns through letters to the editors and articles. They were also encouraged to take part in local and regional radio and TV programmes. Whilst receiving a small grant of some £30 each to get them started, they were expected to raise their own funds locally, no other financial support being given to them from the centre. As the referendum date approached, 374 local groups had been established and, under the guidance of the regional organisers, they were active in preparing for and getting out the vote.

Every conceivable professional and cultural organisation was approached, encouraging their members to set up a group of supporters from their ranks. Thus such groups were formed for solicitors, doctors, authors, actors and other occupations and professions. Posters of well-known supporters from the world of art and sports were printed and displayed. Particularly active were specially formed organisations 'Christians for Europe,' 'Women For Europe' and 'Youth for Europe.' Everyone of their groups had the task of promoting the European cause amongst their peers from the point of view of their professional or sectoral interests.

Shops were rented in prominent positions in several dozen urban centres to assist the distribution of millions of leaflets, pamphlets, posters, campaign buttons, car stickers, window bill and other promotional material. Large widow displays attracted visitors and stocks of the promotional material were freely handed out to all comers for wider distribution.

Each one of the major political parties ran their own campaigns within the general framework agreed by Britain in Europe. Amongst smaller groupings 'Communists for Europe' was set up in opposition to the official Communist party that formed part of the NO campaign. To accommodate the distinct national interests within the United Kingdom, separate organisations were set up for Scotland, Wales and Northern Ireland. To counter the widespread hostility for the EEC amongst the trade unions, several hundred industrial and trading enterprises were encouraged to study the effects of EEC membership on their businesses and then communicate the largely favourable results to their employees.

Mass public meetings were organised throughout the country with prominent politicians and other speakers from professional organisations and universities. Training was provided to assist speakers taking part in daily debates between pros and antis on radio and television. A television film was prepared for screening on the lines of a party political broadcast, which was shown on all channels alongside one produced by the NO campaign. An extensive newspaper advertising campaign was conducted through both the national and regional press, accompanied by a large number of posters displayed on billboards throughout the country. During the last weekend before the referendum, through the encouragement of 'Christians for Europe' sermons were delivered and prayers held in many churches appealing for a YES vote in the referendum. The campaign cost about 2 million pounds and this sum excluded funds raised by the local and professional groups.

The National Referendum Campaign for the NO vote was backed by a number of Labour cabinet ministers who had the government's dispensation to work against its recommendation to approve the renegotiated terms of membership of the EEC and also included politicians like Enoch Powell, Ian Paisley and Tony Benn. They had the support of the majority of the trade union leaders and a number of Conservative MPs, but also the neo-fascist National Front and the Communist Party. Although their motivations against membership were often quite divergent, they presented a unanimous front using the same arguments. It may be that the uniformity of the views expressed lacked credibility amongst the electorate and that is why they lost support during the course of the campaign. Their financial resources were much more modest than those of the YES campaigners, largely because they had difficulties in finding support from business, most of which backed Britain in Europe. They spent about £250,000 including the £125,000 government grant.

60 per cent of the electorate participated in the referendum, held on June 6, of whom 60 per cent voted Yes and 33 per cent for the No proposition.

Lessons for the next referendum

The tasks of those campaigning in favour of the Euro are likely to be harder than it was for the YES campaign in 1975 although, due to the volatility of public opinion on European issues, a strong lead by the newly elected government is likely to help. The economic issues should not present greater difficulties this time round, but much more emphasis is likely to be given by the opponents to arguments about the loss of national sovereignty and the dangers of an emerging European 'super-state.' The opponents will have much bigger financial resources, already promised by wealthy contributors and probably the support of the majority of the National press, although newspaper reading has declined since the 1970s. The nature of the whole debate promises to be heavily influenced by nationalist and xenophobic sentiments of many of the opponents.

To win the case for the Euro it will be important to extend the debate well beyond arguments in its favour. British membership of the European Union and pressure but its other leading members for further integration will come under attack. The 1975 referendum was held some 2.5 years after our entry into the EEC and the Yes campaign was conducted in favour of the status quo under the slogan 'Keep Britain in Europe.' The adoption of the Euro requires a vote in favour of change, which is harder to achieve. On the other hand the labour government recommending the Euro will be fully united unlike its predecessor in 1975, and will be backed by the party. The Conservatives are more divided between Euro-enthusiasts, sceptics and outright opponents of British membership of the European Union.

The actual planning and conduct of the campaign by the current Britain in Europe organisation could do well to replicate some of the strategy adopted by the its namesake in the 1975 referendum. The essential feature of the latter's success was to speak with many diverse voices in favour, each constituent group arguing the case from its own distinct interest. Equally important could be the grass roots activities of local groups of supported, well-guided regional organisers acting under central control. Organisers will have to take into account the new factors affecting campaigning – the increased influence of multiple channel television, the emergence of web sites, the fall in newspaper readership, and the current practice of 'news' management by political leaders. The battle is likely to be fierce but, given early and thorough preparations, it can be won.

Chapter 4

A win-win Game

by Lord David Simon

Editor's Commentary

*The majority of contributors to this book write from the standpoint of experience in one particular area, whether it be as an economist, politician or trade unionist. **David Simon** brings the experience of two different roles: three decades in business with BP, and two years as a Minister in the first Tony Blair Government of 1997. His article poses, with balance and clarity, the fundamental questions which the referendum campaign will address. His conclusions are equally measured and clear: Britain needs to be at the heart of Europe in order to help meet the challenges of change and shape its future. He asks, can we be there without joining the euro? This to my mind is one of the key questions, addressed and answered in different ways in the subsequent articles.*

A win-win Game

by Lord David Simon

The Euro debate is at the centre of a complex of arguments surrounding the merits – or otherwise – of the developing relationship between the UK and its partners within the European Union. Many who are assailed by the daily views of journalists and television commentators – not to speak of our politicians – will want to reflect in their own time on both the political and economic arguments being put for and against the closer union which the single currency exemplifies and possible British membership highlights.

The challenge is broad, beyond the simple question, should Britain join the Euro and EMU? Will joining mean a greater loss of economic and political sovereignty than most understand or would support? Is a continuous unchanging economic sovereignty a real option for the UK in the world of the Internet and free world-wide capital markets? Is political sovereignty worth maintaining at the expense of economic performance – including potential job losses, influence on supra-regional policies in Europe and a stronger shared voice in world economic policies? What chance have we going it alone? Can Britain join Nafta and better protect 15 per cent of its trade in an Anglo-Saxon Club whilst taking a chance on the 50 per cent we undertake with our European partners? Does ever-closer union in Europe mean a German dominated political structure with the Euro as its cornerstone? Are we in the UK really European?

These questions are posed daily in our media and answers pour forth with greater or lesser dogmatic fervour depending – usually – on the editorial line. But many people will try to make up their minds without obvious party political bias.

The history of the UK's relationship with our European partners from the beginnings of the 1970s through the referendum in 1975 to the votes in Parliament on the Single European Act and the Maastricht and

Amsterdam Treaties has been based on a broad cross-party coalition. This political construct has mirrored the way people still appear to think and feel about the European Union and, in a different context, the single currency. On the latter subject one of our parties does seem considerably divided, although it has real supporters within its ranks.

To be frank the British do not necessarily like, or at least are nervous about, the idea of an increasingly integrated Europe, and yet, and herein lies the irony, surveys suggest that they expect and want the UK to be part of the Union, and eventually even expect to become members of the eurozone. Robert Worcester's introduction to this book offers clear insights into this complex mindset. We treasure our memories of past greatness but are pragmatic enough to see that tomorrow's world needs changed attitudes and political structure to underpin economic progress.

Some even see the European Union as a guarantor of social progress and a catalyst for a 'fairer' construction of political decision making in a globalising marketplace. For each of these optimists filled with hope, there probably is a sceptic who says that European politics are opaque and practitioners unaccountable. Electorates are dwindling, malpractice flourishes and over-regulation and expensive labour practices should never be allowed to spread to British shores. You pay your money for 'attitude' and you certainly have all the rhetoric to take your choice.

My own views on the European Union have been fashioned from more than 35 years doing business on the Continent of Europe for BP. For many of those years I lived and worked regularly abroad. I was lucky enough to have been taught languages well at an early age. This certainly helped me to live in communities in a fuller way. For some years I had responsibility for dealing with the European Commission in Brussels on BP's behalf. Through these experiences I have built up a view of the strength and weakness of the Union and the UK's role in it. My life on business has inevitably led to a greater concentration on business and industry than on politics. However, two years as a minister of European Trade and Competitiveness have broadened out my views are built on commercial and political experience and on living in three countries in the Union and visiting all the others.

All told my experiences have been positive. My respect and understanding of out partners motives and aspirations for the Union has increased over time. Whilst there are certainly cultural differences and legitimate disagreements on political structures and economic policies, the overriding conclusions I have drawn, are that that the Common Market and the Community have developed towards a Union over my lifetime because the people and the leadership see the importance of protecting peace and prosperity for the future of their families and communities. They look forward positively because of the political and economic process has brought them benefits.

Of course the balance between European Governance and national democratic institutions needs watching – The Council which we elect democratically through our national polls to select our Prime Minister, the European Parliament elected sadly by a minority of voting Citizens, and the appointed Commission all need reform, modernisation and cleverer accountability. But they do a job that National Parliaments cannot do as efficiently. They guarantee a stronger voice for Europe on an increasingly vital and volatile world stage.

I believe Europe will remain a Europe of Nations. But at the same time it is vital that Europe creates and supports competent institutions and representatives to champion our ideals and economic interest to the World audience. Europe has always been strong on ideas and suggestions to be strong to help solve problems. For example, regulation of world markets is becoming a more urgent challenge. Only with a strong European voice will the USA, Japan and the NECs be convinces to reform and create a business environment, which we can support as free and fair.

I believe these views I hold are general principles, it is not because I have shirked the detail of numerous negotiations on the economic issues facing the UK and our European partners. These details on the advantages of the single market – its strengths and weaknesses on construct – and the vital contribution that the single currency can make to increasing the competitive performance of the Europe's business are all vital building blocks to an understanding of the conclusions I have drawn above. Without understanding the building blocks it is hard to conclude that the house will stand firmly. My experience says that our partners want peace and prosperity as much as we do and so not take inordinate risks when their futures are at stake. They have constructed with care.

The single market and the Euro will bring benefits of stability of investment and low inflation to the members. The stability pact is a continuous and sensible guarantor of fiscal discipline. The crucial legal basis to the rules of the market will be up held by the European Competitions Directorate and the Courts. This is a framework which is sound. Of course there are the famous political wobbles but the foundations for fair trade and improved competition are there, Business and consumers cannot ignore them.

For the consumer better quality products and services at more attractive prices have been the justification for the Single Market and this will continue to be the driving objective. For the UK to avoid the competitive clarity of a single currency if it can meet the tests of convergence and flexibility would seem strangely defensive. Businessmen would regret the reduction of market access. Our wealth creators whether in services or manufacturing, want to be judged by their performance on a level playing field in world markets. Succeeding in Europe and helping to open world markets will be an important step for most of them, as long as the UK can sustain business competitiveness. What better way then competing head to head, one market, one currency and a clear choice for the consumer in Europe, the largest consumer marketplace in the World? The freedom to devalue the currency may be attractive to the political elite and economists, but businessmen and jobholders should beware of relying on clipping the currency, it was never a policy of strength. Our politicians never admitted how slippery was this slope for thirty years. Our current lower productivity performance compared to Germany and France is the inheritance of much past Sterling volatility and subsequent reduced investment. This can happen again – there is no guarantee of currency stability for the UK outside the Euro.

My commercial spirit says 'let's go for it' in Europe. We can gain bigger markets and out compete our partners. This is not a win-lose game: it can be win-win. Why?

It is mostly win-win because we have agreed to build a larger community. Moving the Single Market and the Union boundaries towards the East. We shall in the next ten years include another ten countries at least and 140 million new European Citizens and shoppers.

The political project will underpin growing peace and prosperity for all the community. So that is why it can be win-win for 500 million Europeans. Not an easy win. But then we should think back and remember how hard Spain and Portugal have had to work to become effective members of the Union in the last decade and a half. What a success the Union has been for them and for Ireland. For these countries, membership and greater industrial and political integration has proved beneficial to both citizens and visitors – commercial and leisure. How do we in the UK draw for this evidence, often personally experienced in our way of doing things? We mistrust change yet we see world changing very quickly around us. Political alignments thrown in the air in a decade: Economic growth threatened by regional crises. The USA powering forward. The Internet creating companies within a short five years larger than BP, a huge company, was after 80 years as a leading oil giant. This is an incredible time for change. Technology, politics, life styles, companies all reassembling themselves apparently within months let alone years.

Do we want to shape these changes with our European Partners? Of course we do. We do not want to retreat from the many challenges. I would like to see us committed to reshaping out European society as well as the UK, to take best advantage of these extraordinary opportunities. We have had fifty years of peace and prosperity, inventing and developing a European political structure, which is unique. We can better preserve our long protected natural heritage in these islands, and still help to create better European Institutions to represent our voice across the world. This is the real point of Britain being at the heart of Europe.

Can we be there without joining the Euro?

Chapter 5

No to the Euro

Lord Peter Shore

Editor's Commentary

*Opposition to joining the Euro springs from a number of sources, political and economic, and this variety is well represented by the different contributors to this volume. Some are not against British membership of the EU but oppose the further step of integrating the pound with the euro. Others have consistently opposed the whole idea of Britain in Europe. One of the most constant and steadfast voices against British membership has been and is **Peter Shore**, a member of Harold Wilson's Cabinet during and after renegotiation of the terms of entry, and a leader of the campaign for a negative vote in the 1975 referendum.*

This time he scents victory: he points to the enormity of the task for the government in convincing voters in a referendum on either economic or political grounds. He lays great stress on the Treaty requirement of a two-year period in the European Exchange Rate Mechanism before joining the single currency – interestingly, a point not brought out in other contributions, but mentioned by Neil Kinnock in his concluding interview. He is particularly critical of the Government's claim that joining the euro is overwhelmingly an economic decision, when for most European leaders it is primarily a political ambition.

No to the Euro

Lord Peter Shore

Getting Britain into the Euro is beginning to look as unlikely an accomplishment as that which faces the rich man seeking to enter the Kingdom of God: it would be easier to get a camel through the eye of a needle!

No one should underestimate the longing, the yearning of our Downing Street 'residents' – Brown as well as Blair – to achieve just that and to arrive at last, through the gateway of the Euro into that secular paradise, 'the heart of Europe.'

But the obstacles are huge – not in Parliament, of course, where the defeatism and sycophancy remain numerically so strong even after the June General Election but in the country at large where – and how they must regret it – the Government is pledged to hold a referendum and thus put the issue of abandoning sterling and adopting the Euro to the votes of close on 40 million of their fellow countrymen. In order to win, the very minimum requirement the europhiles have to meet is first to convince a majority of voters that there is a lasting economic benefit for them and the UK if they vote 'Yes' (and serious penalties if they vote 'No') and second that there are not other major non-economic consequences of membership that they would wish most ardently to avoid.

First then to the economic argument, in all conscience, not an easy case to make. The negative argument they fear is that we might be the victims of some form of discrimination by our EU partners or by investors worldwide – has already been frequently rehearsed and is now largely exhausted. It is, after all, some eleven years since serious debate, in the context of the Maastricht Treaty, began to be focused on the Single Currency and it is now more than two-and-a half years since it was formally launched on 1 January 1999. We are not in it and the heavens have not fallen in. On the contrary, the experience of the UK and its people has been almost exactly opposite to what the fearful predicted. The UK did, with considerable reluctance, take the necessary preliminary step for adopting the Euro by joining the Exchange Rate Mechanism in October 1990 and paid a heavy price in mounting bankruptcies, rising unemployment and loss of gold and dollar reserves before being compelled to withdraw in September 1992. But since then the UK economy has enjoyed some 8 years of recovery, of falling unemployment and of economic growth – the longest period of uninterrupted progress since the Second World War. Two particular anxieties loudly stressed by the europhiles as dire warnings of what might happen to Britain if we were left behind our European Partners in abolishing our currency, simply failed to materialise. The City of London, far from losing out to the new European Central Bank and financial centre in Frankfurt, has continued to prosper and of course since January 1999 to buy and sell Euros as it does all other main currencies. Second, the inflow into the UK of funds from the rest of the world has continued unabated so that the UK remains the favoured location for the investors worldwide, far outstripping its European neighbours.

The only real problem that has emerged is in some sectors of manufacturing industry. Some firms have been forced to close plants, particularly in the automobile, shipbuilding, electronic components and steel industries and some overseas investors, particularly some Japanese companies, have warned that unless they can regain profitability, they would be forced to relocate on the continent. But the cause of this simply reflects one of the major oddities of the Government's conduct of monetary and economic affairs. The decision, taken within days of the formation of the new Labour Government in May 1997, to grant the Bank of England a large measure of autonomy in the conduct of monetary affairs, with only an inflation target to guide interest rate policy and with no guidance on the management of the exchange rate, made British exports very vulnerable to the downward slide of the Euro, immediately following its January 1999 launch. Indeed, in the 12 months that followed the launch of the Euro, sterling appreciated over 12 per cent against the new currency thus raising the price of UK exports, lowering the price of European imports and reducing profitability.

True, the misalignment of exchange rates did not deter the inward flow of investment in new manufacturing industry and overall, UK manufacturing exports have held up remarkably well. But there is little doubt that the degree of uncompetitiveness that has been inflicted upon UK industry could easily have been reduced by an active, instead of a passive, exchange rate policy for the pound.

If the American downturn does result in a serious recession and this is communicated to Europe, there will be further closures in the UK – and in mainland Europe. No doubt this will be attributed by the Europhile, however unconvincingly, to the UK's non-membership of the Single Currency. But the really big distortion, that 3 million jobs would be directly at risk if we didn't join, has been exposed and largely demolished in the debates of the past three years.

It is difficult to believe that this job scare could carry much weight now in a referendum campaign. More subtle and perhaps more dangerous are those voices and pens in the media, endlessly suggesting that somehow the UK has shrunk so far from its former imperial might, that it is now a powerless, off-shore island facing stagnation and isolation, unless it abandons along with its frontiers and its independent foreign policy, its own currency.

To that now familiar self-depreciation and defeatism, ever present in the journals of the Lib/Lab intellectual establishment and in so many of the programmes of the News and Current Affairs Department of the BBC, there are several responses. First, that we are one of some 190 separate sovereign nation states, members of the United Nations. In terms of the economic power we rank fifth in the size and wealth of our economy; we are one of the five permanent and veto wielding members of the Security Council of the UN; we are the founder state and still a leading member of the 54-strong Commonwealth with a presence in every continent in the world; and we are a leading member of the 19 strong NATO Alliance. In addition we have security and alliance relations with the United States that are indeed of a special kind and a diplomatic reach and influence unequalled by another European nation state. Furthermore we have a military capacity, nuclear and conventional, that places us in the first rank of military powers.

And if we still have doubts as to whether, with all these assets, we are somehow able to survive, to prosper and to exert influence in the world unless we joint he Euro – let us recall that as recently as the Autumn of 2000, a mere 5-million Danes said 'NEJ' in their referendum and further that in February of this year 7 million Swiss voted against even discussing their country becoming a member of the European Union!

So much for the negative arguments – for the arguments based on fear. But what are the positive arguments for the UK to merge its own currency with the Euro, the currency now adopted by 12 of our fellow Member States in the European Union? No doubt the advocates of membership will discover arguments that have so far eluded me. But the most serious one that I have so far met is that concerned with the exchange rate stability and the contribution to the goal which the Euro will make. Of course, in so far as the European Union states trade with the rest of the world, there will still be the ups and downs of exchange rate movements of the Euro against the dollar the yen the pound and many other lesser currencies. But what is true is that trade within the European Union - now accounting for close on 60 per cent of Member States total trade - will no longer be affected by the movements of national currencies which in the past were due to short-term speculation or to changes in the medium term in the relative economic performance of Member States. Such stability is certainly valued by business, large and small, and is of particular help in planning export strategies of investment programmes – and particularly so when global money markets, political uncertainties and external economic shocks can cause violent and disruptive movements in prices and currency values.

But of there is one thing that business, large and small, values at least as highly as it does stability in exchange rates, it is competitiveness. An uncompetitive exchange rate reduces profitability and sales and, if sustained, leads to contraction of output and employment – and ultimately to closure.

At the moment of entry to a Single Currency, participating states will either have already achieved or will seek the necessary exchange rate adjustment to ensure that it is competitive.

Of course. But the real problem with a Single Currency is not being competitive at the moment of entry but at being able to sustain that competitiveness over the years and decades that lie ahead. If there is one clear lesson that economic history teaches us it is that different countries differ markedly, one from the other, over the years in terms of economic growth and progress. Unless the different countries that form a Single Currency have so closely converged their economies that they have virtually a single economy to go along with a single currency, then gradually their relative performance – their productivity, their competitiveness, their efficacy – will diverge. And if the countries or areas or regions of relative weakness and lower growth are not somehow assisted, then they will stagnate, lose employment, investment and people. The principle means of adjustment of between nation states with differing and changing levels of efficiency is through currency exchange rate movement; appreciation and revaluation af the currencies of the better performing economies, depreciation and devaluation of the currencies of the weaker economies.

This vital adjustment mechanism has been available, throughout modern history, to all states. In the long period of the gold standard, currencies re-valued or devalued against gold; in the decades that followed the Second World War, the IMF policed and assisted what was then described as a regime of 'fixed but adjustable' exchange rates; and when that collapsed in 1973 it was replaced in part by the 'exchange rate mechanism' for 'fixed but adjustable' exchange rates between the countries of the European Community and more likely by a regime of floating exchange rates determined mainly by market forces.

Currency regimes have come and gone but no state over the past century has failed to make not just one but several adjustments – up and down – in its exchange rate to meet the changing relative fortunes of its economy. The exchange rate and its movements are indeed a vital tool of economic management. Without them – without a currency – there is an inevitable and virtually irreplaceable loss of management of the national economy.

That indeed if the price which, in their abandonment of the Franc, the D Mark, the Lira, the Peseta and the rest, the eleven – now twelve – Member States of Euroland have been prepared to pay in their adoption of the Euro as from 1 January 1999. More will be said about the reasons for this decision later. But to continue the economic argument as coolly and objectively as possible, the view of two very senior and experienced Central Bankers on the implications of their decision are worth quoting. Eddie George, Governor of the Bank of England, in his Churchill Memorial Lecture as long ago as 1995 made the crucial point: without the adjustment mechanism of the exchange rate, the only alternatives were 'the possibility of migration of areas of high unemployment to areas of low unemployment' and/or 'pressure for larger financial fiscal transfers from countries with lower unemployment to countries where unemployment was higher.' As he properly concluded neither 'on present evidence looks likely to be particularly effective' – a judgement shared by his colleague and contemporary Hans Tietmeyer, President of the Bundesbank who dismissed the prospect of large-scale transfers from prosperous to less prosperous areas with the observation that 'what is possible within a nation state [...] is hardly realisable between nations' – thus leading him, understandably, to the conclusion with the other participating countries permanently.'

If the loss of the exchange rate as the crucial adjustments mechanism to retain or restore competitiveness was not enough, adoption of the Single Currency is only part of a still larger package of measures involved in the entry to the final and third stage of Economic and Monetary Union. The next key component in EMU if the transfer of control over national interest rates – and mortgage rates - from central banks to the new European Central Bank in Frankfurt. That body, with its treaty guarantees of independence from both national governments and European institutions and its monetarist imperative to give control of inflation overriding priority over every other goal of economic policy, now determines the bank rate and associated interest rates throughout euroland – regardless of the different economic circumstances, that pertain. Whether one region or nation is in deep recession and declining and another is in clear boom, the same single interest rate has to be imposed and endured.

In euroland, National Central Banks – and that will included the Bank of England should we decide to join – no longer determine monetary policy, no longer provide governments with borrowing facilities, cannot even issue currency and bank notes but have become mere branch offices of the Central European Bank in Frankfurt. Whether the interest rate that the ECB president and his council collectively decide is right for the EU will, at the same time, also be right for the UK is indeed a great uncertainty. It cannot be assumed. Finally as part of the EMU package, the Frankfurt Central Bank must be fortified and equipped with reserves so that it can if necessary defend the rate of the Euro against other currencies and can play the traditional Central Bank role of currency market interventions, loan guarantees etc. which was formally played by the now impotent national central banks. And to do this, the ECB must be able to conscript such currency reserves as its role requires it to play. So far Member States in total have been required to contribute an initial 50 billion Euro. Individual contributions have been calculated according to a key based in the main on GDP and population. Since the UK is roughly equal to France in both respects, our contribution would be of the same order: 16 per cent of the total, or some £5 billion.

The arguments of stability apart, two other allegedly positive consequences of Single Currency are usually deployed. First that the transaction costs which formerly were incurred in exchanging one European currency for another are no longer imposed. Since the Commission itself claims that this accounts for not more than one-half of one percent of GDP and in the case of the UK, with is generally more efficient banking system considerably less – perhaps as little as 0.1 per cent of GDP, this is hardly a major consideration. And in terms of consumer convenience, the credit card performs for the majority of travellers and tourists, virtually the same function as a common currency. The second claim is that a single currency will promote price competitiveness. It is true that prices thorough-out Europe formerly denoted in national currencies and soon to be replaced by the Euro will make it easier for people to make comparisons as to price advantage. But most people, certainly when they are considering major purchases, are perfectly capable of making meaningful comparisons of relative prices even when they are quoted in foreign currency denominations. Clearly, UK shoppers crossing the Channel to visit French supermarkets have done their sums!

For what it is worth, these general arguments about the merits and demerits of joining the Single Currency, have been supplemented by the Chancellor in the definitive statement of Government policy that he made on 25 October 1997 when he assured us that he would only recommend joining the Euro if the economic benefit was 'clear and unambiguous.' In assessing this, our helpful Chancellor listed some five conditions that needed to be met before it was safe to join: sustainable convergence of the UK economy with those of the other EU states; sufficient flexibility for the UK to cope with future economic change; positive effect on business investment in the UK; favourable impact on our financial services industry and the business conducted by the City of London; finally that joining would be good for employment. Only when the Chancellor and the Treasury assessed that these five tests have been met will they recommend membership to Cabinet colleagues, to Parliament and the Nation. Commentators and critics have asserted that these test are largely subjective and that the Chancellor could at any time declare they had been met and the whole exercise is geared not so much to measuring convergence with the economy of the European Union as with measuring the state of British public opinion about joining the Euro as revealed in successive opinion polls. What is certainly true is that only some of the Chancellor's tests are capable of objective measurement. That would include comparative interest rates, inflation rates and unemployment rates but nobody could pretend that for example, the 'flexibility' criterion is capable of anything other than opinion. But the really crucial tests – the ones we have already discussed about the loss of the main instruments of nations economic management. The exchange rate and interest rates and their implications – do not even feature in Brown's list. As aids for helping to assess the wisdom of joining, his five tests are therefore virtually worthless.

Nevertheless the exercise does serve a purpose: first it does give the Government some room for manoeuvre as to the timing of the application for membership; and second it does help promote the image of a Government, despite its enthusiasm for all things European, yet refusing to be tempted by the pressures for premature application, only making its move when a grave voice chancellor, baggy eyed with late night studies of the minutiae of the economy, emerges from No.11 to tell the waiting world that now at last it is safe to proceed!

Even so, and with all the aids and props of spin and PR, the Chancellor's task is truly Herculean. He and his Cabinet colleagues have to convince the nation not just that there is a case and an argument for membership but that to repeat the words of Brown's October 1997 statement, the economic benefits for Britain are 'clear and unambiguous.'

In recent debates and commenting the UK on the Euro one of the oddities has been that while discussion has continued with some intensity of the Chancellors five conditions, very little has been said about the other five conditions, those laid down in the Maastricht Treaty and its related Protocol, governing the conditions that must be met by any applicant nation, seeking to join the Euro. They too are focused on what the Treaty calls 'sustainable convergence' and the criteria cited are price stability, budgetary balance, long term interest rates and exchange rate stability. The fifth condition is legislation to ensure that central banks are made independent of national control and rendered subordinate to the ECB.

In the four years of New Labour's rule the Government has followed meticulously the Treaty requirements almost savagely adopting as 'golden rules' the fiscal policy, public expenditure and public borrowing rules and recommendations of the Commission, the ECB and Ecofin. No problems should therefore arise on the European side should the UK make its application for membership.

There is potentially one major hitch, the Treaty condition concerning exchange rate stability. According to Article 109J of the Maastricht Treaty and its amplifying Protocol on the Convergence Criteria, exchange rate stability has to be judged by the performance of an applicant currency in a two-year period of membership of the Exchange Rate Mechanism (ERM) prior to application. Furthermore, that currency has to observe the normal fluctuation margin around parity, '2.5 per cent,' and there has to be no devaluation against a European currency during that period.

The UK is not a member of the ERM and the earlier experience of membership from 1990 to 1992 traumatised not only the Treasury but the leadership of both the main political parties. Far from meeting the condition laid down in the Treaty and rejoining the ERM, the Chancellor – and his colleagues – have gone out of their way to state and restate that they have no intention whatever of doing so.

Does it matter? Astonishingly, no one is able to give a clear nor authoritative answer. The Government – and its predecessor – point to the fact that since the Maastricht Treaty and its Protocol were written and as part of the launch preparations of the Euro in January 1999, a new ERM has been created as from that date with slightly different rules: in particular with more permissive margins of 15 per cent on either side of parity.

When questioned in the House of Commons, the Prime Minister has implied that these minor changes have somehow removed the basic tests of exchange rate stability – the two-year membership, without devaluation against a European currency. As he put it: 'there is no Treaty obligation for Member States to put their currencies into an exchange rate mechanism.' To underpin his claim he has quoted from the Resolution on EMU agreed at the June 1997 Amsterdam meeting of the European Council, in particular paragraph 1.6 of Annex 2 which states: 'participation in the exchange rate mechanism will be voluntary for the Member States outside the Euro area.'

Voluntary? Correct – so far as it goes! The Prime Minister does not make it clear whether these words – which certainly apply to a Member State with a derogation, one not seeking to join the Euro – still apply to a Member State which has made an application to join. The last two sentences of 1.6 only add to the uncertainty. They read: 'nevertheless,

Member States with a derogation can be expected to join to the mechanism. A Member State which does not participate form the outset in the Exchange Rate Mechanism may participate at a later date.'

Would the UK therefore be 'expected' to join the mechanism? There is some evidence to suggest that the Government would like to claim that these words do not apply to the UK since the UK's own Protocol (no.11) is not so much a derogation as an opt-out! This however is not convincing – if only because Article 10(a) of the UK Protocol implicitly admits that our opt-out should be treated as a derogation.

So far, the only experience of a Member State seeking to join after the 11 launched the Euro in January 1999 is that of Greece, which applied for membership in early 2000. Greece had joined the ERM two years earlier and the procedure followed was precisely that laid down in Article 109J of the Maastricht Treaty and its related Protocol.

One further consideration. In the UK's own Protocol No.11, Article 10A clearly states that:

> 'the UK shall have the right to move to the third stage provided only that it satisfies the necessary conditions. The council, acting at the request of the United Kingdom and under the conditions and in accordance with the procedure laid down in Article 109K(2) of this Treaty (which reaffirms the procedures and requirements of Article 109J shall decide whether it fulfils the necessary conditions.'

So: will the UK have to join the new ERM or if not the Chancellor, the Cabinet, parliament and the majority of voters decide to apply for a Single Currency membership? The Government say No – and anyway that it will not do so. The Commission has said yes on at least one occasion but along with the ECB, Ecofin and the rest has maintained a more or less complete silence on the issue.

The Treasury Select Committee in its report on the EMU in July 2000 tried to establish the facts. The economic Secretary to the Treasury, Melanie Johnson, flatly stated that: 'we have an agreement that we should not have to do that and we have absolutely no intention of being in an ERMII or shadowing the Euro or any other such agreement' – but failed to give Chapter and verse as to what the 'agreement' was. We can only assume that she was referring to the statement in para 1:6 of Annex 2 of the Council's Resolution of June 1997 that joining ERMII was a voluntary activity. Not surprisingly, the Select Committee concluded that: 'it is not clear whether the UK will be required to join' ERMII or whether: 'a period of exchange rate stability outside of ERMII would do.'

This is an astonishing admission. Of course the operating assumption in the Treasury and the FCO and in the minds of Ministers may well have been that the Member States and the institutions of the European Union were as pantlingly keen for the UK to join the Euro as they are to abandon sterling and to adopt the Single Currency – so much so that the UK would be allowed to flout at least one of the Treaty conditions

No doubt some Member States still are ready to be accommodating. But the fact of the matter is: the UK application would need to undergo rigorous examination and win a favourable appraisal, from both the Central European Bank and the European Commission. It would then need a formal positive recommendation by the Commission to be upheld by Ecofin and finally to be approved by the heads of Governments, meeting in the European Council.

That procedure is clearly laid down in the Treaties and no one has sought to challenge it. Thus in both Ecofin and the European Council the UK application could be challenged and would require, on a vote, the approval of a qualified majority. Finally – and most dangerously – the actual rate at which the pound sterling was exchanged for the Euro would have to be agreed. Here again the procedure to be followed is laid down in the UK's own Protocol, in paragraphs 10C. It is that we would accept and follow the procedure laid down in the Treaty Article 109L(5). And this state that the commission, having consulted the ECB, will propose the rate at which the pound would be 'irrevocably fixed' in terms of the Euro – and this proposal will be adopted by the council 'acting with the unanimity of the Member States' of Euroland.

The Unanimity! Here indeed is room for mischief. A competitive rate would be crucial. The UK would be a lonely, naked demandeur, desperate to win acceptance and inclusion, vulnerable to every demand made upon it in all the wide areas of the Treaties where the UK is in conflict with its fellow Members States.

A truly nightmare prospect!

One final problem. Just when is that 'irreversible conversion rate' for turning the pound into the Euro to be agreed? The Treaties procedures clearly imply that it would be the final decision of the European Council itself in a process of examination by the Institutions of the European Union that would have begun with an application to join. In other words the irrevocable conversion rate would not be known when the referendum campaign took place and indeed some period – weeks, perhaps months – after a Yes vote had been obtained. For many advocates of membership – certainly for job anxious trade unionists and for most of the TUC General Council – lowering the high uncompetitive present level of sterling against the Euro is the main reason for supporting entry.

Unless therefore the 'irreversible conversion rate' is known and declared before the referendum votes are counted, the sponsors of the Yes campaign would be asking the electorate to buy a pig-in-the-poke: to put their trust in the skill and wisdom of those in Downing Street and in the goodwill of their colleagues and competitors in the European Union.

So far we have dealt only with the first of the Government's essential requirements: their need to give ample proof to the British people that joining the Single Currency would be, in the Chancellor's own words, 'clearly and unambiguously' in our economic interest. But we stated at the start, a second requirement, at least the equal and in the judgement of many of still greater importance, than the first: a need to demonstrate and persuade the British people that there are not lined and adverse political and constitutional consequences of joining the Single Currency: that there is not a non-economic price in terms of loss of our democracy, our self-government and out sovereignty that most British people will never consent to pay.

And it is precisely at this point that the real falseness and emptiness of the Government's position becomes plain. Consider: of joining the Euro, as the Government asserts, is overwhelmingly an economic decision, why on earth should it be made subject to that virtually unique procedure, the referendum? No other economic decision, be it a budget, the introduction of a new tax, the nationalisation or denationalisation of the Bank of England, joining the ERM, floating the currency, devaluing the pound, has ever been subject to such a procedure. The referendum, virtually unknown in UK practice until recent years, has been severely limited in its use to precisely those major constitutional and institutional issues which concern Government itself: to cite the most important, the referendum on remaining within the Common Market in 1975, the referendum's held on Scottish and Welsh Devolution and on the Government of Greater London.

So why a referendum if the issue of joining the Euro is simply economic?

Consider further what it is that has motivated and persuaded the Governments of the 12 states that now that comprise Euroland, to abandon their Central Banks and currencies and with them, the major instruments of national economic policy, exchange rate and bank rate and transfer them to a new, untried European institution, the European Central Bank? As we shall see, it was overwhelmingly the political not the economic argument.

Or consider in particular the case of Germany. Does anyone, with even the slightest knowledge of that country, believe that Germany, proud possessor of the strongest currency of Europe, the D Mark – which has come to be the very symbol of German Post-War achievement and revival – agreed to surrender the D Mark and replace it with the Euro in the belief that there would be economic gain and greater exchange rate stability! Ludicrous.

The Governments of the Euroland states no doubt had a variety of reasons that it was the political, not the economic arguments that swayed them. They knew very well that, having surrendered the main macro-economic powers of the nation state, there would have to be a compensating growth of power and decision making in the supranatural institutions of the Union. For them, not something to be feared but to be welcomed. Few would disagree with Hans Tietmeyer, President of the Bundesbank's statement that 'the European currency will lead to Member States transferring their sovereignty in fiscal and wages policies as well as in monetary affairs. It is an illusion to think that states can hold out their autonomy over taxation.'

The authority of the Commission and of the economic ministers meeting in Ecofin has been greatly extended over the whole conduct of economic policy and the drive for the harmonisation of indirect taxes, on both consumers and corporations – and delayed by the British – will now, under Nice Treaty rules facilitating 'enhanced co-operation,' go ahead.

On all this, there is an open agenda thoughout the Continent. In 1992, the year when the negotiations for the Maastricht Treaty were finally completed, the goals of the EMU and the Single Currency established in the text of the Union Treaty which in its own words, 'marks a new stage in the process of creating an even closer union among the peoples of Europe,' European leaders felt able to celebrate their achievement publically. Chancellor Kohl, then the most powerful voice in Europe spoke for the most when he asserted: 'in Maastricht we laid the foundation stone for the completion of the European Union [...] which in a few years will lead to the creation of what the founding fathers of modern Europe dreamed after the last war: the United States of Europe.'

That, or something very close to it is the great ambition that lies behind the creation of Euroland. Indeed, far from the pursuit of economic gain, during the years that separated signing the Maastricht Treaty in 1992 and actually launching the Euro in 1999, the Member States accepted policies of fierce deflation – cutting public expenditure, reducing borrowing, raising taxation in order to achieve the degree of convergence and the targets for inflation and borrowing laid down within the Treaty. For some seven years the founding members of Euroland endured an unemployment rate of over 10 per cent and economic growth which averaged only 1.8 per cent

When at last agreement among the eleven in May 1998 to launch the Euro as from January 1999 was finally achieved, it released a veritable chorus of celebratory prose focused not just upon the political achievement but on the significance for closer political union.

If the testimony of so many national leaders is not enough, perhaps this unequivocal assertion by the first president of the ECB will convince: 'EMU is and always was meant to be a stepping stone on the way to a United Europe.'

What, then, are we to make of the Blair/Brown pretence that the Single Currency is primarily an economic issue; that we should judge the case for membership in terms of the arithmetic, the pluses and minuses of economic gain; that, in Brown's words in the 27 October 1997 statement of government policy, 'the constitutional issue is a factor in the decision, but it is not an overriding one'? Are we to believe that everyone in Europe has got it wrong, and only the British have got it right? Sounds a bit insular, even xenophobic, to me!

Since both men are highly intelligent, the usual explanation of Ministerial misjudgements and errors – lack of information, pressure of events – cannot be deployed. They do not know what the constitutional and political implications of the Euro are. They are prepared to see the UK democracy drained of its power of economic management. They are prepared to push this still free people and this self-governing state, into a kind of Babylonian capital inside the European Union, with the power to make the policies that affect us and the laws that we must obey in our own land transferred to unelected and foreign officials in Brussels and Frankfurt.

They will not, because they dare not, face the nation with the reality of their European enterprise: the creation of a single European state. They know very well that the British people, with all the goodwill they have towards their Continental neighbours, nevertheless believe that the great prize and possession of democratic self-government must never be surrendered.

So far, although the issue was repeatedly but ineffectively pressed during the June 7th General Election campaign, the Government has managed to avoid serious public discussion of the political and constitutional implications of the Single Currency. But this will not be possible when the decision to join is made and several weeks of intense, focused debate commences.

The Government can scarcely look forward to this event. Time is running out if a decision is to be made in the new Parliament since, as the Government itself has agreed, a decision will have to be made 'early,' or within the first two years after the General Election.

Opinion has been regularly polled over many years. But, in the near decade, since the Single Currency proposal emerged in the Maastricht negotiations, not one UK opinion poll has recorded a majority on favour of membership. MORI, which has regularly polled since 1991 and posed the question: 'are you in favour?,' reports that, in the long pre-launch period from 1991 to 1998, never have those in favour exceeded 33 per cent while those against have averaged 55 per cent, ranging from 49 per cent of the lowest to 64 per cent of the highest. The 'don't knows' have never exceeded 20 per cent. Since the Euro was launched, MORI polls have indicated an increase in hostility to the Euro.

Clearly a big switch of public opinion about the Euro is required if Blair and Brown are able to reach their goal. It can be argued that opinion is still, shallowly rooted; that once a Government, with all the authority that high office confers, clearly states that it is in the national interest to join, opinion will be powerfully affected. Didn't that happen in the two to three months that preceded the only other European referendum, the one conducted in May 1975?

It did: and as an active protagonist, a Dissenting Minister I well recall the unfolding events. The crucial factors were the unanimity of the media in favour of Britain's membership of the EC. Not one of the daily or Sunday national newspaper – other than the Communist Party's Morning Star – supported the No campaign. Secondly, the fiction was maintained that there were three parties in the debate: the No campaign, the Yes campaign and independently the Government! So, since the Government was strongly advocating a Yes vote, the built in imbalance was, from the start, two to one – which mattered particularly in the literature sent out, under a free post, to every elector.

Third, there were then virtually no rule lay down to guide the conduct of referendums. In particular, there were no financial ceilings on expenditure. Money – mainly from the Business community poured into the Yes campaign and into full-page advertisements in press, and posters on hoardings nation-wide. Professional staffs, skilled in public relations, advertising and the media, produced daily briefings for press, radio and TV and helped to organise newsworthy 'events.' The Yes campaign outstripped the No campaign by something like 12 to 1.

The issues were of course represented – falsely – as economic ones: that Britain was joining what was primarily a trading club and that it was in the interests of British Industry and economy to do so. The political content of Rome and other Treaties was indeed addressed by the No campaign but its voice was drowned by the megaphone voices of the national press

This time it is likely to be very different. The conduct of elections and referendum in the UK and the financing of political parties were the subjects of enquiry by the Neil Committee on Standards in Public Life in 1998 and a number of major changes were recommended and subsequently legislated for by the Government and Parliament.

The new and independent Electoral Commission will certainly be involved in devising the rules of the game and in supervising their operation. There will be no 'third party' in the referendum – only the Yes and No campaigns. The BBC in spite of its scarcely disguised europhile tilt, will be obliged during the campaign period itself to be strictly impartial!

But the most significant change is in the media. Far from the unanimity of 1975, the national press is now virtually evenly balanced, with champions on both sides of the debate in both the popular and the broad-sheet press.

There are still legitimate reasons for concern. In spite of the Neil Committee's recommendation that foreign money – whether corporate or individual – should be banned form the British electoral process, the Government has deliberately exempted companies based in the European Union.

Nevertheless, the prospect is very different from that which faced us in 1975. With an economic argument that is almost contemptibly weak, with a political purpose of a federal type union that cannot be argued because the country won't have it, with a Government forced to dissemble and cheat but which cannot be successfully conceal, with 'partners' in Europe able to exact a penal price for admission, the chances of success are not great. A British understatement! If challenged to place a bet, I would put my money on that Biblical camel getting through the eye of the needle sooner than our Europhile Government will succeed in its endeavour to enter the secular paradise of euroland.

Chapter 6

Joining the Euro

by Sir Roy Denman

Editor's Commentary

*It is hard to see how the Government or other proponents of entry can continue to duck the political questions when one thing that unites the hard rock opponents and those who fear for Britain's future influence outside the monetary system is the certainty that it is a political issue. One person who is in no doubt on this score is **Roy Denman**, our most experienced international trade negotiator. He has been as consistent in his views and activities in favour of British involvement in Europe as his one-time Minister Peter Shore has been opposed. He has been tireless in his criticism of the failure of British politicians over forty years to understand the postwar movement of continental political opinion.*

He is also one of the few proponents of joining the Euro to have the intellectual courage openly to face up to what he sees as the inevitable consequence of the single currency – some form of political union. But, he argues, Britain outside claiming to play a leading role in Europe would be a fantasy.

Joining the Euro

by Sir Roy Denman

Should Britain join the Euro? This is the most important decision facing the country for the last half century. Two factors set the frame of any discussion. The first is that the question is not the abstract one of the desirability of an economic and monetary union for Europe. The great majority of our European partners have already decided to embark on one. The question is whether we join them or remain aloof.

The second is that the question is not simply an economic one. The Government's policy implies this. It declared in 1997 that Britain should in principle join Europe's single currency, if the Euro proved a success and if membership were shown by certain economic tests to be in Britain's best interests. The balance of economic interest is clearly a very important factor. No sensible person would want to embark on an enterprise likely to end in bankrupcy. Even if it seemed reasonably likely to end in success certain wider political considerations would be involved. But first let us consider the economic balance of advantage.

The Governor of the Bank of England, no advocate of Britain joining a single currency, nevertheless summed up in a lecture in 1995 the case for considering this option:

> 'If asked why we should be contemplating a move to monetary union, the economic - as distinct from the possible political answer - would have to be that the permanent elimination of exchange rate fluctuations between the member states would promote economic prosperity within Europe by increasing further the benefits to be derived from a single market.'

These benefits would come in a variety of forms. Travellers would benefit from the absence of exchange rate costs and uncertainties. Business transaction costs would be reduced. Big companies can normally keep these low and cope with short term currency risk, but small and medium-sized enterprises have to pay a bigger share of their profits for currency transactions. Greater price transparency would benefit consumers; without a citizen in country X having to use a pocket calculator to find the equivalent price in country Y, there would be downward pressure on prices. A single currency would mean greater capital mobility throughout the union, and a more uniform pricing of risk would improve the efficiency with which capital is allocated. Interest rates would be lower. And investment would be encouraged by the absence of exchange risk in a union of 300 million people which does more than four-fifths of its trade internally. Conversely, investors would have less interest in a Britain subject to the hazards of a daily fluctuating exchange rate against the Euro.

But those who doubt the advisability of our joining a single currency focus on other issues. They argue that a one-size-fits- all interest rate would not fit Britain because the UK economy is out of step with the rest of Europe. Unexpected shocks and downturns in the economy can now be met by altering interest rates and the exchange rate. Within the eurozone these would not be available. One alternative would be intra-European fiscal transfers which, to be effective, would have to be backed by federal taxes unacceptably high. Another would be adjustments to wages and prices. But are these flexible enough to take the strain? The UK has a much greater sensitivity to short term interest rates than the eurozone because both households and companies have a relatively large amount of borrowing at floating interest rates. Interest rate changes therefore are more likely in the UK to lead to boom or bust. And the preeminence of the City of London in world financial markets hardly needs the adoption of a single currency; indeed its activities could be handicapped by Continental overregulation.

Faced with a choice between these considerations, the tests the Government has said that they would apply after this year's election number five:

1. Are business and economic cycles in the EU and the UK compatible so we can live with the same interest rates as the rest of the eurozone?
2. Is there sufficient flexibility in labour markets?
3. Would joining the single currency create better conditions for firms making longterm decisions to invest in Britain?
4. What impact would entry into the eurozone have on the UK's financial services industry?
5. Will joining the Euro promote higher growth, stability and a lasting increase in employment?

Most of these tests allow considerable scope for judgement. In some the single currency is not the only factor. The position of the City of London as Europe's leading financial centre depends in part on factors such as London's attractiveness as a city and the cluster of existing companies. The UK's popularity among overseas investors owe much to the English language, lower social costs and flexible labour markets.

The fundamental questions about joining the Euro relate to convergence of interest rates and business cycles. In 1997 the Treasury took the view that Britain's economic cycle tended to be closer to that of the US than to Europe. But Britain and the eurozone are now at similar points in their economic cycles. According to the National Institute for Economic and Social Research both economies are expected to grow this year at little less than 3 per cent. And following the cut on February 5 of UK interest rates, at 5.75 per cent they are only one per cent above Eurozone rates. Sterling is above its longterm equilibrium exchange rate but not by much. And British inflation, currently 0.9 per cent, is not only the lowest in the EU but less than half the eurozone average.

Two other developments since 1997 are also worthy of note. One is some evidence of greater wage and price flexibility. The fall in the number of people out of work and claiming benefits without setting off a surge in pay suggests that the labour market has become significantly more flexible. And the fact that British companies have coped with a rising exchange rate by cutting prices shows that prices can adjust without creating recession.

The second concerns investment. Those who doubt the benefits of joining the Euro point to the huge preponderance of Britain's share of inward investment in the EU in 1998 despite its being outside the eurozone. But some major Japanese companies have made it clear that if Britain were to remain outside the Eurozone for a substantial period of years, they would have to consider relocating investments elsewhere. Thus, whatever the favourable current figures, the risk of a major future loss of inward investment is a real one.

The result is a fairly wide agreement among economic commentators that the Government's five tests have very largely been met. Both the National Institute of Economic and Social Research and Professor Tim Congdon, a wellknown City expert and avowed Eurosceptic, concur. But this does not close the debate. Economics is not an exact science, it is an affair not just of calculation but of intuition, psychology and uncertainty.

And views on economic issues are often influenced by other factors. The Government's eventual view is bound to depend on whether it thinks a referendum on the Euro is winnable. Many will be influenced by political considerations. Indeed the the choice is fundamentally political. There are two reasons for this; one relates to the political past, the other to the future.

The creation of a single European currency is merely one stage in a historical evolution that began in 1950. which is nothing less than one of the great revolutions in world history, the creation of a European federation that would promote the prosperity of its citizens by sweeping away divisions of currency and trade and which could better defend their interests in the world by speaking with one voice. The movement began with the proposal in 1950 of Robert Schuman, the Foreign Minister of France, for the pooling of the coal and steel industries of Europe. His declaration made it clear in terms that the 'pooling of coal and steel production will immediately provide for the setting up of common bases for economic development as a first step in the federation of Europe.' A further step was the Treaty of Rome (1957) which established a customs union. The first President of the European Commission, Walter Hallstein, charted the future of his Europe in three lapidary phrases, 'Customs union, economic union, political union.' The move to a single currency can only be understood in this context.

With very few exceptions British politicians failed to understand this seismic shift in Continental Europe. For them the Second World War was a great and glorious victory, with Vera Lynn singing 'There'll always be an England' and Spitfires circling over Dover. For the Continentals the war was a long, humiliating disaster. Jean Monnet understood the difference when he came to London in 1950 and tried and failed to persuade Sir Stafford Cripps, the Chancellor of the Exchequer, to join the Coal and Steel Community. He wrote later 'England had known neither defeat nor occupation. She had no need to exorcise the past.' For the Continentals a federation was the only secure means of bridling extreme nationalism should it ever recur and threaten to repeat the horrors of the past. Moreover for the eurozone countries a federation is a defence not just against the troubles of the past but the economic dangers of the future. The logical end of a customs union is some form of political union.

A report on customs unions drawn up by the League of Nations between the wars had this to say: 'For a customs union to exist, it is necessary to allow free movement of goods within a union. For a customs union to be a reality it is necessary to allow free movement of persons. For a customs union to be stable it is necessary to maintain free exchangeability of currency and stable exchange rates within the union. This implies inter alia movement of capital within the union. When there is free movement of goods, persons and capital in any area, diverse economic policies concerned with maintaining economoic activity cannot be pursued. To assure uniformity of policy some political mechanism is required. The greater the interference of the state in economic life, the greater must be the political integration within the union.'

Thus, for reasons linked both to political aims and economic self-preservation, the Euro is likely to be followed by some form of political union, in plain English, a federation. The precise form this will take is not yet known; it is bound to be the subject of long and arduous discussion. Again this prospect is widely misunderstood in Britain. The impression is widespread that some quite sensible plans for freeing trade in Europe have been hijacked by power-hungry bureaucrats in Brussels and turned into a plan for a Superstate. Any European who had ever lived in the German Federal Republic or the Swiss Confederation would burst into laughter at such a thought. When cities or states make common cause they need to respect in their actions the interests of the others. When Ireland objected in February this year to strictures from other eurozone ministers on its budgetary policy, one commentator wryly recalled that when the Stability Pact was agreed unanimously some years ago the then Irish Minister of Finance had defended it on the grounds that when everyone was drawing cheques on a joint account there needed to be some agreement on what they were withdrawing.

So the fundamental question is not whether Britain changes the colour and format of its banknotes but whether it is prepared to join in the further political and economic integration of Europe.

We have considered the economic risks of joining. There are those who argue that we have no need to consider any such risks. Britain, with its successful economic performance over the last ten years could do well enough on its own.

The figures tell a different tale. The British employment record compares well with the rest of Europe but this is offset by poor productivity performance. British productivity is 9 per cent below the EU average, 11 per cent below the German, 15 per cent below the French and 21 per cent below the Italian. British performance is even worse in terms of productivity per hour because working hours are longer in the UK than in other major countries. Partly this reflects low levels of capital investment. To be sure we have risen from 11th to 10th place in the EU league for GDP per head of population, but even then we are about to be overtaken by Ireland. And in GDP per person employed we are 13th out of 15 members, behind Spain and ahead of only Portugal and Greece.These perspectives offer scant comfort for the view that on its own Britain could become the Hong Kong of Europe.

There are also risks if we do not join.

Particularly from 1 January 2001 when the Euro enters circulation and becomes for the man in the street a reality, there is bound to be steady pressure for economic coordination within the eurozone. This will not mean that levels of taxation will be identical throughout the area, any more than this obtains in those successful federations, Switzerland and the United States. But the differences should not be such as to endanger the stability of the common currency. Indeed international discussions on financial issues will increasingly take place between the US, the eurozone and Japan. Britain will have no effective role in this, nor will it be able to influence eurozone decisions which will affect the UK economy. A club is usually open to non members if invited for social occasions but decisions about its affairs are limited to those who have paid their subscription to become members.

Britain's decision to exclude itself from the eurozone could have further consequences. The rest of the EU might well argue that if Britain was essentially interested only in a trading arrangement then less time would be wasted at Council meetings if Britain (and possibly Sweden and Denmark) were given associate status like Norway, simply implying a free trade agreement and nothing more. This would mean, after the Norwegian example, that free trade would be limited to non-agricultural goods and that associate states would have to accept without discussion trade regulations passed in Brussels.

A further consequence relates to exchange rates. Between the US and the eurozone sterling could be expected to bob up and down like a small boat between two ocean liners. If sterling appreciated sharply British exports to the Eurozone would come under great pressure. If sterling were forced into a substantial devaluation against the Euro there would be howls of protest from eurozone manufacturers about unfair competition from a country which had free access to their market but which was not bound as they were by a single rate of exchange. Action could take the form of a compensatory surcharge by the eurozone against British exports. This could be justified under Article 5 of the Treaty of Rome on the grounds that the disruption caused by devaluation was 'jeopardising the attainment of the objectives of the Treaty.' Retaliation by Britain would be counterproductive since over half British exports of goods go the eurozone compared with only 7 per cent of Eurozone exports destined for Britain

Britain's exclusion would not be limited to economic questions. It will not be long before the questions facing the regular meetings of eurozone finance ministers become such that a summit is necessary. Heads of Government, once assembled, are not likely to restrict their discussions simply to economic questions. Political decisions will also be taken, all the more as the eurozone progresses to political union. Britain will thus be increasingly cut off from the decisions taken over a widening front by a uniting Europe. Any claim that Britain is playing a 'leading role in Europe' will be seen as fantasy.

A further consideration is a longer term one. Over the last fifty years Britain's relationship with Europe has been marked by a steady refusal to believe that integration would ever happen, that if it did happen it would not work, and then after many years a grudging acceptance of a framework which we had no hand in devising. In 1950 when the Coal and Steel Community was proposed we not only held aloof but made it clear that we did not think it would work. It did. When it was followed by plans for a European customs union our representative walked out of the preparatory discussions for what was to become the Treaty of Rome with the famous words, 'The future treaty which you are discussing has no chance of being agreed; if it was agreed, it would have no chance of being ratified, and if it were ratified, it would have no chance of being applied. And if it were applied it would be totally unacceptable to Britain.' Eighteen years later Britain accepted the treaty in full.

The same pattern looks like repeating itself. When the Delors Committee came up in 1989 with its detailed recommendations for a single currency, Nigel Lawson, the then Chancellor of the Exchequer damned it as 'incompatible with independent sovereign states with control over their own fiscal and monetary policies.' Britain made it clear that it did not expect economic and monetary union to come to pass. Disobligingly it did. Not surprisingly, since no British government has ever encouraged a full debate on the pros and cons, public opinion is now massively against the UK adopting the Euro. But interestingly the public expects Britain to join in the longer term. A MORI poll in November 2000 found that despite current opposition, 61 per cent expected Britain to have adopted the Euro by 2010, even more (66 per cent) by 2015. Joining earlier would mean having a voice in fashioning the political union which will follow the single currency instead of just, as in the past, tamely accepting later what others had drafted.

It is of course objected that joining the Euro means giving up sovereignty. NATO and the GATT (now the WTO) have constricted our freedom of action for half a century and the EU Treaties for almost as long. Where was our sovereignty when we were forced into the devaluation of 1990? Sharing a common currency with a bloc of 300 million others would give us prospects of stability, increased investment and growth far greater than on our own. The economic risks of joining are generally thought to be substantially less than they were four years ago. The economic risks of staying out remain subtantial.

But the fundamental choice is political. What future does Britain see for itself? On its own it would be a negligible player in the world, a sort of flyover country on the edge of a powerful, thriving European Federation. On the other hand a Britain genuinely committed to building an integrated Europe would be in a far different position. Buttressed by the English language and all its historic links across the seven seas, a Britain representing a commonly agreed Union view could play a leading role both in Europe and in the world. That is the challenge.

Chapter 7

Does the Retention of our Currency Matter?
'Not a tuppenny damn'

by Nigel Farage MEP

Editor's Commentary

*Surprisingly, perhaps, root and branch opponents of British membership of the whole European project such as **Nigel Farage** would agree with much of Roy Denman's fundamental political analysis. He parts company on not wanting to have anything to do with the Euro – or indeed the EU - precisely for the political reasons which compel the previous contributor to the opposite conclusions. Unlike some other opponents of losing the pound, however, Nigel Farage is not a romantic about our currency: he believes the strength of the notion of nationhood will lead to the break-up of the EU and the people will rediscover that small is beautiful.*

Does the retention of our currency matter? 'Not a tuppenny damn'

by Nigel Farage MEP

Oh, there will be a degree of cultural impoverishment, as with all standardisation and homogenisation, but we have already lost the crown, the florin, the ducat, the tanner, the doubloon, the sou and many other denominations, yet still our children sing a song of sixpence and plead that we place a penny, a halfpenny or a farthing in the old man's hat, still we offer a penny for your thoughts and talk of making silk purses our of sousieres, and still tuppenny damns are worth precisely tuppence, if that.

The currency is a decoy and a distraction. Yes, my party has made much of keeping the British pound sterling no less than the pound imperial, but for reasons entirely practical, not sentimental. There are short-term problems. First, and admittedly temporarily, the cost of converting to the Euro will be devastating. Second, the sheer enormity of the scope for counterfeiters with an unfamiliar currency and no border controls will deliver a crippling blow to the already ailing newborn currency.

For all that, at the last, it matters not what we call the units of our national currency, but merely that we have a national currency and thus control over our national destiny. The right to set interest-rates and to impose taxes in response to national needs and aspirations is fundamental to democratic government, and the 'harmonisation' of taxes and interest rates by an unelected, and therefore unaccountable, body is at once inequitable and ecologically destructive.

I use the word 'ecologically' advisedly. Not only is there an ecology of cultures, ideas and special interests which depends for its health and sustainability on diversity, but a 'one size fits all' economic policy which regards, say, Slovakia's needs as identical with Italy's can only be sustained by the total obedience of all member states and of all their citizens to a master plan.

If, then, there are ordained regions of monoculture - here Europe's cereal-growing area, here Europe's livestock farm, here her dairy - each is dependent on the other and it is in the interests of one to sustain the other. If, however, as is traditional, there is economic, social and ecological diversity and consequent self-sufficiency within each member state, the economic requirements of each at any given time will be widely divergent.

In short, as with any system run by a vast bureaucracy, the EU can function only if it is, in the truest sense, inhuman and unnatural, if all natural anomalies and sports, all regional differences, all initiatives yielding profits to particular areas, are ironed out. Federal Europe can be a capitalist trading bloc only by enforcing the communism of nations. It is as damaging to human and cultural ecology - and, incidentally, that of the landscape - as would be a well-meaning, anthropomorphic programme to ensure the health of prey animals by hobbling their predators.

Federalists invariably cite the United States as a model for their great experiment. It is a specious and spurious model. Not only was the Union established by consensus where the EU has been established by prolonged deceit and *force majeure*, but the many people of many nations who colonised the United States were united against the unsettled and hostile terrain and the native population. They brought their European cultures and loyalties with them but in large measure subsumed them as they joined forces to form a new nation, a new race with one predominant language and one predominant loyalty. The EU seeks to subsume established interests, customs, cultures and loyalties to a common cause.

It will, it must fail.

This is not wishful thinking. If for a moment I believed that the Federal dream could be realised without loss of justice and democratic self-governance and that nation would coo unto nation in perpetuity, I would invest my energies into realising that dream. Alas, not only is there no evidence to support such a notion, but all the evidence proves that it is misguided and doomed to failure, and that the attempt to mould disparate nations into a harmonious unit will and must entail gross repression, intrusion and curtailment of liberties.

Before we dismiss nations as outdated and irrelevant, it were as well that we explore the nature and purpose, the raison d'etre of nationhood. What is a nation? It is a geographical unit, of course, identified by culture, climate, custom and costume and bounded, frequently, by seas, rivers, ranges of mountains or hills or other natural barriers to casual traffic. On other occasions, however, there are no such immediately obvious boundaries. Then boundaries are determined by conflict and established by treaty or force of arms. Nationhood cannot be determined by outsiders. Anthropologists and all just thinkers are agreed that a people is what it believes itself to be.

Why, then (teleologically rather than mechanistically), should there be such things as nations in an age in which tribal or clan associations with localities are memories only and when modern travel laughs at mountain-ranges and oceans? Why should the world be riven into countless nation states, some large, some tiny, all convinced that they possess a unique shared identity and interests distinct from, if not inevitably inimical to, those of their neighbours?

Globalists and idealists, often well-meaning if naive, posit a world in which there are no such boundaries, no such loyalties - the anodyne world of John Lennon's *Imagine*, with no possessions, religions or nations and all the people 'living life in peace.' Unfortunately, to attain any such state of affairs, it would first be necessary to erase the human genome and start afresh, eradicating such inconveniences as lust, the territorial imperative, acquisitiveness, philoprogenitiveness and even creativity. Again, the attempt to create any such world would entail totalitarian control and repression and would be doomed to failure. Again, it would be as ecologically vandalistic as genetically modifying all species to homogeneity.

Not only are nations, with their complex identifying cultures and constructs, precious artefacts worthy of preservation in themselves, but they exist because they fulfil a vital human need which has not been denied by even the most ambitious and radical of social engineers.

Morality unrelated to self-interest is meaningless and so cannot survive. From the first social contract, 'I won't kill you as you sleep provided that you will not kill me,' reciprocity for mutual benefit is at the heart of our ethics and our laws. Initially, and for good genetic reason, extended to families, then tribes, then nations, it identifies an 'us,' a group to which we owe and from which we demand in turn allegiance and obligations.

Just as a form is defined by the space surrounding it, so an 'us' is defined by a 'them.' Without so manifest a link between self-interest and morality, morality and law become mere, vague notions of 'niceness' which nature plainly scorns. The 'nice,' the 'selfless' and the law-abiding plainly do not thrive in a unit which does not reward such virtues. It is therefore equally logically provident to revert to pure self-interest.

A nation, identified by language and tradition, thus marks the outer imits of responsibility and sympathy, which is why it will always and inevitably reassert its identity as an 'us' to which we belong and which affords us strength, as opposed to a 'them.' Upon the notion of nationhood depends, at the last, all persuasive or sustainable morality, all practicable law.

Every artificial construct intended to subsume nationhood has failed and broken up, usually amidst bloodshed, as component parts of Unions and Empires reasserted their identities and demanded self-determination. The Holy Roman Empire and its imitator under Napoleon disintegrated, not randomly, but into nations. The latest to emulate that Justinian model, the EU, will suffer the same fate. The Austro-Hungarian Empire, the USSR, the Warsaw Pact, even Tito's little Yugoslavia - all were megalomaniac jigsaws which broke up and went back into the box, albeit grievously shop-soiled and damaged, in the same shapes as those in which they had arrived.

That the EU will break up, then, is not moot. There is no historical model for such a Union enduring whilst there are many for its dissolution. The only question, therefore, is whether we wish to see our children or grandchildren battling for self-determination against a Euro-army, or whether we, with the example of history clearly before us, will quietly and peaceably renegotiate a free-trade agreement with the EU now - which, after all, is what the British people were promised - and retain our freedoms and our right to determine our island's peculiar destiny.

Our 'special relationship' with the US has seen peace maintained for nearly sixty years. This is not to say that that relationship is perfect (none is). It is, however, to say that the American and British styles of democracy and the liberties of the individual are founded upon something far more fundamental than fashion, and that the Napoleonic or Justinian model, whereby the people exist to justify the ever-fatter State (whereas, under Common Law, the foundation of all great democracies, the State exists to serve the people), we are sib, as with all our Commonwealth cousins.

The British people fought a long and bloody war amongst ourselves. as, indeed, did the Americans, to establish that extraordinary, subtle and complex mechanism of checks and balances which sees the people as sovereign, the sovereign representative of the perpetual freedoms of the people and Parliament our transitory servants, responsible only for representing our transitory views.

The model of EU government is very different. Not only is there no effective democratic rule in Brussels and Strasbourg (a debate in which the average length of speech is 90 seconds is hardly worthy of the name, nor a parliament whose members are powerless to initiate law), but the extraordinary judgement in the case of Bernard Connolly, dismissed by the Commission for criticising its corruption and its ineffectuality, demonstrates that that populocentric, or democratic model has actually been turned on its head.

Pleading that his freedom of speech had been infringed, Connolly was astounded to hear the judgement that, on the contrary, he had infringed the 'human right' of the EU to govern by presuming to criticise it. This is terrifying stuff - the reintroduction, in effect, of the law of seditious libel, a tool of dictators through the ages which presumes that the people are mere functionaries of the State as opposed to its masters.

The British system has been the model for countless democracies throughout the world, yet our politicians, acting without popular mandate, are readying themselves to sacrifice it all - for what? For a trading bloc.

Federalist portray themselves as modern visionaries. It is far too seldom observed that the whole notion of the EU is as old hat, as painfully antedeluvian, as absurd today as would be Dame Vera Lynn strutting her stuff in a thong and thigh length boots on *Top of the Pops*.

Trading blocs belong to another era, when there was not free world trade, when there was a constant threat of belligerence from continental Europe, when the USSR was in its pomp. It was then that, to the likes of Edward Heath, the cause of world peace seemed well served by a European trading bloc punching well above the weight of its constituent states. That illusion tallied well with the ambitions of other European nations yet smarting from defeat or 'liberation' at the hands of the Allies, and with the Americans' understandable desire to create a buffer zone between themselves and the Communist East.

All that has changed. The Communist Soviet has shattered into a hundred, nation-shaped pieces and abandoned its Marxist doctrines. Trade is now truly worldwide and nigh instantaneous, and the game is open to anyone willing to play, regardless of size or, save in a very few cases of human rights abuse, allegiances.

It is as though, in a world of laptops, we were striving to reconstruct Charles Babbage's first, giant 'analytical engine,' as though, with speed records falling year by year to individual runners, we had reasoned that thirty men strapped reluctantly together must run thirty times faster than one.

Switzerland thrives without a cartel. Norway continues to trade freely with the world without sacrificing her autonomy or her people's right to self-determination. Both, whilst retaining independence, do proportionately more trade with the EU than does the UK. Even Mexico has a free trade deal with the European Union which will shortly be as good or better than our own, yet has suffered no loss of sovereignty or autonomy in consequence.

Commissioner Neil Kinnock has publicly confirmed that, in the event of our withdrawal, there would be no punitive trade restrictions between Britain and the EU. Since we buy far more from EU countries than we sell to them, this is hardly surprising. All figures snatched out of the air, therefore, such as the 'three and a half million jobs' which, Tony Blair assures us, hang in the balance should we not adopt the single currency, can be quite simply dismissed as nonsensical, scaremongering propaganda without foundation.

On the contrary, our business culture, our fewer regulations and, of course, the English language, have made Britain a magnet for inward investment. We currently receive half of the inward investment attracted by the entire EU. Breaking free of EU constraints and regulations will only increase our lion's share of investment, creating, not destroying jobs, whilst the return to our balance of payments of the £25 million a day which we curently pay into the EU budget can only enhance British industry and enterprise.

It is, of course, a grave mistake to assume that the popular view is necessarily the right one. As the ancient graffito points out, if we followed the example of billions of flies, we would be reduced to eating ordure. In the case of the EU superstate, however, with a common defence policy, a common army and a common currency, the compliance and the support of the populace will be essential to its success.

That compliance and that support are simply not there. The people know that they were dragged into the Union by quite deliberate, insidious deceit. The people quite rightly mistrust the giant bureaucratic monolith which is Brussels. They know of the massive extend of corruption in the Commission and Parliament. They fear the unaccountability of the Commission and the global political ambitions of federalists and economic imperialism of globalists. They resent the loss of control over their own destinies. They will continue to resent the fact that, for example, British fishermen have been put out of a job whilst British money has gone to create jobs and to build a giant Spanish fleet to pillage British waters.

Should pensions be harmonised, they will resent still further the fact that British people are paying for the ever swelling ranks of pensioners in Germany and Italy, for example, where the birthrate is now lower than that of mortality. These resentments will increase, not diminish, as more and more powers are transferred from the nation, and so the people, to an amorphous construct called Europe.

The break-up of the European Union has thus already started before the project has been completed. What can check the non-compliance? Only force or panem circensesque, and force has a poor record in compelling compliance - and that only grudging and rebellious, and for no more than a few years, whilst popular taste in bread and circuses is way, way ahead of that which Emperors will feed the public.

The most staggering single factor that should persuade students of the futility of the European project is the vast discrepancy which exists between supposedly representative politicians and the people, not merely in Britain but in Denmark and, it seems, even in Germany. Polls have consistently shown that the British electorate does not want further integration with Brussels and that many (52 per cent at the last count) would favour immediate withdrawal, yet not one of the principal political parties at Westminster offers that option, nor do the politicians' cronies in the media reflect the anti-EU feeling on the streets.

From this, the logical conclusion to be drawn is that the professional political class is quite plainly not doing the job for which it is elected and employed, but is accepting power from the democratic process, then using it for an undemocratic purpose.

Not only is this morally reprehensible and constitutionally abhorrent, but it demonstrates the carefully fostered class-system upon which the EU depends for its existence.

Sneering, not reason, is a weapon frequently used by the pro-EU, pro-single currency faction. I can, for example, list the EU failures in the UK - the destruction of our fishing industry, the crippling of agriculture, the demise of the steel industry, the ruination of the railways, the decline of democratic representation and so on - all undeniable facts. I stand to be corrected by the arguments of others in this volume, but the usual response is not a matching list of EU benefits to Britain, but rather theoretical ideology without empirical foundation, coupled with the sneering implication that we who oppose Britain's integration are unable to understand what is patently obvious to all intellectuals with large brains and, above all, large incomes.

The Danish campaigners for the single currency even went so far as to assert that the decision as to whether to vote 'Ja' or 'Nej' was, at the last, simply a matter of intellect. The Danes, to their eternal credit, rejected this condescending drivel.

It is with shame that I assert it, but I assert it nonetheless: were every MP in Parliament debarred from taking office or monies from Brussels for life, over 50 per cent of MPs would be fighting for the restitution of power to the British Parliament, whereas at present none is, because the earnings, allowances, perks and prestige awaiting loyal advocates of European integration when they retire to the privileged impotence of the Brussels parliament.

The privilege is extraordinary, the expenditure profligate. From the moment that I arrive at Strasbourg airport, where I am whisked along a special MEPs' lane to a waiting limousine, I am flattered, fawned upon and invited to an orgy of champagne receptions and the like. My travel expenses far exceed my travel costs, but I am encouraged to pocket them nonetheless. My lavish secretarial allowances can go to anyone that I choose, with no scrutiny as to the recipient's secretarial skills. There is even a giant MEPs' hypermarket where I can buy everything from Mercedes to mink, tax and duty free.

Is it any wonder that MEPs, though soon aware that they have no power to change the lives of their constituents for the better, are content to furnish the veneer of democratic process to the vast, unresponsive bureaucracy, headed by the unelected Commission, which is the EU?

That word 'unresponsive' is of vital importance. Small government is nimble and yare. In Britain in 2001, we saw how cumbersome and slow to the tiller is that vast tanker moored in Brussels. When confronted by the plague of foot and mouth disease which threatened the entire rural and tourist economy, Britain was unable to act autonomously to save British interests. Her Ministers must go cap in hand to Brussels to seek permission to take action which, scientists agreed, must above all be taken quickly.

Experts agree that culled carcasses should be buried in quicklime in situ and as fast as possible. Others advised ring-fencing outbreaks by vaccination, again, as a matter of urgency. EU legislation, however, forbad both these measures. In order to implement these policies, therefore, government had first to submit their requests to the Commission, who must in turn heed the decision of the Standing Veterinary Committee (SVC), which must attain a qualified majority of 62 votes out of 87 in order to approve any initiative.

In the meantime, as the chief veterinary officers of fifteen nations argued amongst themselves and delivered their verdicts which were then converted to grudging and excessively cautious Commission Decisions, hundreds of thousands of carcasses lay bloated, bursting and suppurating virus into the air in British farmyards, often for three weeks or more, at once spreading the disease, destroying Britain's reputation as a tourist resort and, incidentally, causing horror and trauma to the many families confined to their premises with their stock lying dead and rotting all about them.

Whatever the deceptions and misrepresentations from on high, at the last, the people will have their say. They always do. The rebellion may not start in Britain, but it will come. Will we then see Euro-tanks in the streets of Copenhagen or London as once we saw Soviet tanks in Czechoslovakia, imposing 'support' of a detested regime? Or will it be sufficient that each member state will be dependent upon others and therefore can simply be starved into submission? Either way, I can see precisely no point in taking such a risk and surrendering autonomy when we could as well trade freely with Europe and the world without any such surrender.

The multi-nationals favour the Euro. Britain's small businesses have overwhelmingly voted not only to reject it but to withdraw from the EU. The politicians to a man or woman favour further integration, with, as we have seen, good (or, rather, sound), if undemocratic reason.

The people favour recovering small-is-beautiful government - self-determination and democracy. They are right to do so.

Chapter 8

Why we must win the fight for the Euro

by John Stevens

Editor's Commentary

In a country such as ours noted, even by unsympathetic outsiders, for a political tolerance and moderation not unconnected with a relatively consensual and usually non-ideological approach to major questions, the European debate arouses extreme passions. Not extremist in the sense of far left or far right, but almost a battle for the English soul over Europe which the two main political parties have not always been able to contain. I say English because the Irish, Welsh and particularly Scottish bodies politic seem to have been less deeply affected.

One result has been the frequent dramatic swings between the enthusiasts and the sceptics in British representation in the European Parliament since the first direct elections in 1979, often out of kilter with broader political trends reflected in Westminster. Nigel Farage in 1999 represented an upswing in the anti-European mood on the right from which the pro-Europeans in the Conservative party suffered, among them John Stevens, one of their leaders for ten years in Strasbourg. There could be no greater contrast in their political views of Britain's future; at least this volume provides a forum for both if neither Strasbourg nor Westminster does, and our debate is richer for it. John Stevens particularly takes on the Atlanticists who favour an American alternative to Europe; as Editor I have been interested in how relatively few opponents or sceptics of Britain's future in Europe actually seem enthusiastic about NAFTA as a realistic option. However, as a former diplomat who always disagreed with Talleyrand's admonition 'surtout pas trop de zèle,' I salute the passion with which John Stevens argues his case.

Why we must win the fight for the Euro in Britain

by John Stevens

For nearly two generations now, Britain has been in the grip of a growing identity crisis. Are we Europeans or are we not? Are we closer to America and the rest of the English speaking world across the seas, the 'Anglosphere,' or to our continental neighbours? The only other European country to have, in any way to the same degree, such a deep internal dispute about whether her destiny is in or out of Europe is Russia, a disconcerting companion.

Everywhere one turns, in our economy, in our society, in our general culture, this rift is plainly apparent. It underpins all other debates in our politics. We agonize over the future of our public health and education systems, yet what we are seeking are European levels of provision with American levels of taxation, an impossibility. We speak the language of American-style flexible labour markets, but our attitudes to risk and mobility are far closer to European practice. We dream of an American-style entrepreneurial economy without having their entrepreneurial culture. We talk about how we are becoming a multicultural society like America, but we are still deeply attached to European-style notions of what constitutes nationality.

Successive British governments have sought to present this schizophrenia as a strength, as getting the best of both worlds, none more so than the present one. If the 'Third Way' means anything, it is the apotheosis of 'The bridge across the Atlantic' mummery. But it is becoming painfully clear that Britain has, in fact, been getting the worst of both worlds.

Our economy has neither the commercial creativity through low taxation, small government and the fostering of an individualistic ethic of America, nor the strategic stability based on high government spending on education and infrastructure, a protective regulatory environment and the fostering of a nationalistic ethic of Germany or France. It is split right down the middle between sectors and firms which are basically dollar or Euro orientated and is thus increasingly incapable of being run coherently.

The Chancellor, who has pledged to avoid boom and bust, is well on the way to achieving both simultaneously. We have allowed our manufacturing sector to decline too far and even in those services, notably international finance, where we have ridden the tiger of globalisation far more effectively than our continental competitors, it has been at the price of losing control completely to overseas interests. Of course, in a boom that does not matter. But in a bust? A severe downsizing of City employment by American and European investment banks, for example, which may be on the cards, would devastate the economy of the South East, the engine of our national wealth creation. Our productivity and our overall levels of investment, in particular our spending on R&D are disappointing, both by American and leading continental standards. So is our per capita GDP. We work longer hours for less pay than any G7 country. Most of these severe structural problems have been masked over the last few years by an exceptionally benign international economic environment. But if that were to change, no major economy is more vulnerable to severe retrenchment than that of Britain.

And our society is neither one which aspires to be blind to ethnic, cultural and regional differences, because they are all dominated by a shared dream of individual self-fulfilment on the American model. Nor one which insists upon the assimilation of diversity within a dominant culture, or its containment within elaborate federal constitutional structures, along continental lines.

Some elements of our deeply divided identity have been around so long they have ceased to occasion outrage, like the crisis in Northern Ireland. Some, like the new assertiveness acquired by Scotland and Wales, through their embryonic devolved governments, are only beginning to exert their potentially powerful centrifugal force upon the fabric of the United Kingdom. But, ironically, it is within England that the fissures are most threatening. The difference between London and the rest of the country is far greater than that between any other dominant or capital city and its hinterland in any major country in the world.

London is in many respects, in its values, its diversity, its ethnic tolerance, in its bizarre mix of private affluence and public squalor, the part of Europe most like America. But the gap between London and, say,

Bradford, dwarfs the differences between Paris and Perpignan, or Berlin and Lindau. It dwarfs even that between New York and Baton Rouge. The much-trumpeted revolt of the countryside, driven by the ongoing collapse of agriculture or the impact of taxation on fuel, is merely the tip of a deep hostility from outlying regions, such as the South-West, towards the centre. The fact that many of its leaders are hobby farmers and sportsmen whose wealth comes from the City and who are seeking in an imaginary rustic idyll some satisfaction of their hunger for belonging, merely shows that even the winners in modern Britain are deeply alienated. Can one imagine the heterodox and confused cast of the 'Countryside Alliance' in America, or in Germany?

Another alarming index of alienation in British society is the increase of racial tensions. In the past, we have been rightly proud of our tolerance towards our non-white minority citizens relative to France and America. Now, elite racism is more pronounced here than in America and we are seeing the younger generation of our former immigrant communities more discontented than their parents, in sharp contrast to developments on the continent.

But perhaps nowhere are the consequences of this failure to define who we and what values bind us together, more poignant, than in the fact that Britain has the highest rate of family breakdown, of teenage pregnancy and of child poverty of any G7 country. Ultimately, even a national identity crisis is a very personal matter.

One can make a coherent case that we should resolve our schizophrenia and heal these dangerous divisions in our economy and our society by wholeheartedly embracing America and her ways. It is the real case against the Euro and against our whole positive engagement in the European Union, not the tortured, fogeyish, recessional romanticism and suppressed xenophobia of the letters columns of the 'Daily Telegraph' or of William Hague's 'Save the Pound' bandwagon. Europe's most serious opponents are those Atlanticists who sincerely believe the peoples of Britain should, like Americans, be bound together by nothing more than the necessarily contingent condition that this is a relatively good place to earn a relatively decent living. Illusions of roots and the enmities to which they give rise should be cast aside, in favour of a growing sense of being at home in the world. They imagine that our economy could prosper as a fully integrated part of the American economic zone, as members of NAFTA and as de facto, and even de jure, users of the dollar. This, in turn, would, they fancy, bring us to the leading edge of the ever-integrating global economy. They do not advocate, nor do they fear, that this would reduce our trade with the European Union. On the contrary, they think we would be better able to operate in Europe as an outpost of the American economy. They wish to reject social democratic welfareism and collective, community responsibility for our neighbours, in favour of private, individual provision. They are convinced that this will release our individual energies and ambitions. In short, they consider all of Britain could and should become like London writ large.

Since the advent of the Bush administration it is a case that has won powerful adherents in Washington. For it is seen as just a part of a far greater, global battle to ensure that the world becomes like America writ large. To this way of thinking, Europe, the European Union, represents a great barrier to progress. It favours intense regional economic integration secured by binding international law, rather than broader global free trade secured by American power. It does not desire growth at almost any price. It wishes to preserve cultural particularism, notably in languages, instead of bowing to an increasingly homogeneous, Americanized global elite culture. Most important, it represents a potential alternative pole of attraction, an alternative model for the developing world, on the way globalisation should proceed, to that of America. And the battle between these American and European models will be fought out in Britain. If we join wholeheartedly the American camp, their global agenda is secure. But if we vote to subsume sterling in the Euro, with all this implies for our commitment to the continent, the days of the worldwide dominance of the dollar, the single most eloquent expression of American power, will be numbered. The stakes could not be higher.

On all this Atlanticists and pro-Europeans can agree. But the outcome of the Euro debate in Britain will not just decide the relative global status of America and Europe. It could also determine whether the European experiment in international integration of the past forty years survives at all. Whereas the Atlanticists here and in Washington have a clear litany of how rigid, over-regulated, protectionist (both externally and internally) and provincial Europe is, how it faces the past not the future, and how catastrophic our embracing of it would be for ourselves and for the world, most stop short of suggesting that the whole edifice might fail. But the other side seem to lack all conviction. Even the elites of the so-called inner core countries of the eurozone seem to show no comparable confidence in the strength of their cause or sense of its global significance. Certainly they are not really proclaiming the advantages of the Euro or of other European developments, like the Nice Treaty, which is why popular support for the whole enterprise is eroding, even in France and Germany.

The introduction of the Euro indeed constitutes an act of high ambition, the most ambitious economic policy ever undertaken in a free society. As the logical extension of the Single Market it was conceived, in part, as a response to 'Eurosclerosis.' And it has already dramatically transformed the pace, depth and breadth of European economic integration. Its most powerful psychological effects in the wider populace will only come with time, as the new notes and coins bed down. But already the disciplines of the Maastricht criteria on government debt, which has effectively capped the share of GDP taken by the public sector, represent a significant shift towards competing head on with American economic liberalism, affecting fiscal, labour and capital market policy. In key sectors, such as telecommunications and aerospace, there is a new determination to exceed American performance. And there is a growing willingness, in areas like trade and the environment, and in defence, to enunciate a distinct European vision and to seek consciously an equality of influence and authority with America. There is some talk of the European Union as a model for Latin America, or Africa, or the Middle East.

But there is also a chronic overall lack of leadership and lack of will. The Euro has not yet brought Europe the capacity to take over the role of locomotive to the world economy from a flagging America. Important reforms that would allow a genuine open market in, for example, corporate control, have stalled. The enlargement process is mired in disputes over labour mobility. The Continentals do not have the British problem of identity: they know they are Europeans. But this had not brought them much closer to knowing what sort of European Union they want or why: a potentially fatal weakness.

If the political will can be generated here to proceed - something that now plainly needs a passionately pro-European opposition to bolster a vacillating and pusillanimous, if still, in principle, positive government - Britain will be the only major European state to test the Euro before the bar of public opinion in a referendum. Of course, the core of our case will be the British national interest. We will show that roots and a sense of community still matter to us. That happiness and fulfilment and meaning in life are to be found not just in individual successes but in the shared advancement of locality, region and nation. That our economy will perform better and our control over the mechanisms which generate our wealth will be far greater if we choose a fuller integration within the adjacent continental single market composed of a number of roughly comparable states than with a far more dominant entity separated from us by three thousand miles of ocean. We will prove that our trade performance with the American economy and with the rest of the world, will be all the better for our having the economies of scale of the European single market as our home base. That it is right to make welfare provision for those in our society who cannot look after themselves. That private and public affluence are allies not enemies. We will demonstrate that the division in these islands can be resolved by a federal constitution which devolves power from London not just to Edinburgh and Cardiff, but to Newcastle, Birmingham, Manchester and other centres. That if we are viscerally hostile to our French and German neighbours we will also find it hard to show genuine respect to our Asian or Caribbean fellow citizens. That our values, in our attitudes to our families and to ourselves, derive ultimately from a common European civilisation, which offers us a sense of continuity with the past without which the future is confounded with a perpetual present and all responsibility in our society is devalued. In short, we will be arguing that we are British not Americans. But when we win, we will have made the case for Europe for the other Europeans as well. We will have revivified the entire enterprise.

We have been in this position before. In the seventeenth century, Britain faced a protracted constitutional crisis which combined profound internal economic social and ethnic divisions with a decisive choice of external orientation, between the Catholic absolutist superpower of Louis XIV's France and the oligarchic Protestant international inspired by Holland. From the triumph of the latter in the Glorious Revolution, we trace not just the British state - which has only now, since the loss of Empire, run its course - but also all modern notions of parliamentary democracy, probably our greatest gift to Europe, America and the world. However much it is vilified by its opponents as undemocratic, the European enterprise is also fundamentally, all about democracy. It is about the democratisation of the new global economy just as much as the imperfect oligarchy voting in Westminster on the Act of Settlement in 1688 was about the democratisation of the then new national economy. The European Union remains the only attempt in the world to forge a fully-fledged international rule of law governed by international democratic processes, principally indirect, in the Council of Ministers, but also direct, in the European Parliament. The heart of our case is that international democracy is possible. The heart of the Atlanticist case, made by the proponents of national parliamentary sovereignty here, or the opponents of extra-territoriality in Congress, is that international democracy is impossible. It is the core of the difference between the European and the American vision of globalisation.

If they are right, then there is no prospect of balancing the great international forces in the world economy with international political processes of comparable reach and power. And that might be the least of our problems. It lays the world open to the rule of the strongest superpower and that might not always be the basically friendly, if flawed, force that is America. If we are right, one dollar, or one Renmimbi one vote will be checked by one person one vote and the structures to secure international liberty and justice will have been pioneered.

Given our history, nothing could be more fitting than that it should fall to us, in seeking to resolve our own profound internal contradictions, to also, once again, carry forward the future of the European identity and of the cause of democracy. Perhaps only when it is understood how great the charge is that we do hold in our hands, will we generate the same intensity of motivation that currently animates our opponents. Perhaps then we will find the fire to make our cause one of such patriotism and vision that there can be no doubting the outcome?

Chapter 9

Trade Unions and the Single Currency

by John Edmonds

Editor's Commentary

Back down to earth, it is important to remember that the European debate in general, and the Euro issue in particular, are about not just high principles but mundane reality as well - jobs, welfare and economic benefit. The contributions in the second half of this book will concentrate a little more, but by no means exclusively, on these aspects while still not losing sight of the political issues. Actual experience of the EU has confirmed some in their hostile views; on the majority trade unions were opposed to Britain in Europe. **John Edmonds** *is a prime example of this change. I do not think it is a coincidence that it has accompanied a much more realistic and forward looking general approach to the protection and promotion of trade union members' interests. There is also to my mind not much point in being a member of the EU if you don't try to learn from others' experiences.*

As a result John Edmonds and many like him see both the political disadvantages, and the risks for the protection of the interests of companies and their work forces, in staying outside the eurozone He also points out that entry into the single currency would strengthen British arguments for EU reform.

Trade Unions and the Single Currency

by John Edmonds

When the indefatigable American trade unionist, Sam Gompers, was asked what trade union members wanted, his answer was terse and confident. 'More,' he declared.

Perhaps it is a sign of the times that nowadays, faced with the same question, trade union leaders refer to the results of opinion polls and focus groups. Since 1984, GMB has used Mori to poll working people regularly about their aspirations. 'What do you want from work?' we ask. People certainly want 'more,' but they do not pick out the bigger pay packets and longer holidays which Gompers had in mind. Top of the league table in the GMB poll is more interesting work and more job security. Pay comes well down the list and fringe benefits come even lower. People want a job which stimulates their mind and frees them from the threat of redundancy.

These findings prompt the questions which trade unionists ask about the single currency. Will it create more jobs? Will the jobs be more secure? Will the jobs be better and more satisfying? Will economic fluctuations be greater or less? Trade unionists want to know whether the single currency will help them to reach their aspirations and to gain more control over their working lives.

Uncertainty

The trouble is that no one, however learned, can confidently predict the outcome of the single currency project. The europhiles tell us that the opportunities are vast and rewarding. They offer the view that greater integration into a massive European trading bloc will generate wealth on a scale so far unknown. Allegedly, our currency will also be protected from the speculation that caused havoc on Devaluation Wednesday. But here is the rub. It was our participation in the Exchange Rate Mechanism which provoked the speculation and the single currency looks very like a more unforgiving version of the ERM. Was the ERM fiasco the result of defects in the mechanism itself, or did we just go in at the wrong rate - a suicide rate, as John Smith memorably called it? The jury is still out.

On the other hand, staying out of the Euro is no longer the soft option it once appeared. Apart from Britain, all of the powerful Member States within the European Union are part of the eurozone. Gordon Brown's failed attempt to secure a seat on Committee X was the first of what is becoming a lengthy series of rebuffs and humiliations. When the Finance Ministers of the European Union meet, there are now two sessions. In the first session the Finance Ministers of the twelve Euro zone countries go through the agenda and decide policy. Gordon Brown is excluded. By the time the formal Council meeting starts and Gordon Brown is invited in, all of the important decisions have been taken. Being outside the single currency means being cut off from the centre of European policy making.

European political leaders are polite people and, for the moment, we are protected from the most damaging results of exclusion by the expectation that we will eventually join. Britain is not exactly courted by the Twelve, but at least they treat us with the care appropriate to a country which might eventually be part of the inner circle. Of course this effect will quickly dissipate if the British Government indicates that entry will be indefinitely delayed. The courtesies will disappear and British economic initiatives will be given even less attention. If - after further delay and recrimination - we eventually decide that entry is inevitable, we will have to adjust to a set of rules which we have had no part in drafting and which take little account of UK interests. These are significant drawbacks and trade unionists should take them seriously.

Euro-sceptics argue that staying out gives us the opportunity to manage our economy without restriction. In reality, the freedom available to refuseniks is greatly exaggerated. The German Finance Minister has long warned that the European Union will not tolerate 'irresponsible behaviour' by EU members outside the eurozone. In practice, any hint that Britain intends to follow a policy of narrow self-interest is likely to produce a very sharp and concerted reaction from Brussels. The BSE debacle demonstrated that there is a host of measures that the EU can use against Britain. The European Union is a massive negotiating council in permanent session and a country which behaves in an anti-communitaire manner on currency issues is likely to find it very difficult to strike a deal on beef, on fish, on company law, or on anything else of significance. At the outset, the policy of opting-out may be trumpeted as a brave assertion of economic sovereignty, but in time, it may well turn into a shabby exercise in expediency with the aim of avoiding retribution from the twelve eurozone members.

Lessons

The last three years have taught British trade unionists that exchange rates are of supreme importance. During a period of strong economic growth, manufacturing industry has been cutting back employment and capacity at a desperate pace. The Labour Government boasts that its first period of office has produced a million jobs. But this net figure conceals a loss of nearly 300,000 jobs in British factories. Most manufacturing companies blame their difficulties on the high value of the pound. In 2000 and 2001, the pound was trading at about 25 per cent above the level justified by the economic fundamentals. Whether the pound would have fallen to a more realistic level if the British Government had announced early entry into the single currency is a matter for debate, but the need to reduce the value of the pound is seen by most trade unionists as a major aim of economic policy in Labour's second term.

The behaviour of British management during the period of crisis has taught trade unionists a second lesson. I had a vivid example of the problem last autumn. Two union members had told me how they were driving to their work at a clothing factory in Leicestershire, when the local radio carried a news flash. Top management had just announced the closure of their factory. There had been no warning and no consultation. That behaviour by Coats Viyella was abominable, but it was in no way exceptional. Vauxhall announced the closure of their Luton plant after giving a series of undertakings about future production. Corus refused any discussion of their problems until top management had made a final and unchangeable decision to close British steel plants. Ford announced the end of assembly work at Dagenham in direct contravention of a written undertaking from top management. Each of these companies was severely criticised, but in spite of the outcry, the closures took effect.

Looking across the Channel, we learn that industrial problems do not have to be tackled in such a brutal fashion. BMW is required by German law to consult worker representatives about major structural change. The Company would not have been allowed to have treated German workers in the way they treated British workers over the intended sale of Rover. Indeed, British trade unionists eventually discovered that BMW had discussed their plans for Rover with German trade unionists well before any British worker had an inkling of BMW's intentions. At every turn, the relative insecurity of British workers is emphasised. When Marks and Spencer tried to use British management tactics to close their Paris store, French law intervened to require the Company to consult properly. Steel plants in Britain have a better productivity record and reach higher quality standards than steel plants in Holland, but when the decision was made by Corus to cut capacity, it was the British plants which were targeted for closure. It is much easier, much quicker, and much cheaper to declare redundancies in Britain than in any other country within the European Union.

Where does this leave the British worker? The single currency may well encourage further industrial restructuring which could further threaten the employment security of British workers who already feel vulnerable. But staying out of the eurozone looks more and more like a policy of political cowardice with few real-life economic advantages. Faced with such inconclusive arguments, trade unions in Britain naturally seek ways of reducing the risks. Some policies can be ruled out immediately. No sensible person advocates entering the single currency at the current high value of the pound. Similarly, no sensible person would opt for a rushed entry without proper preparation. However, following the experience of the last few years, trade unionists have now added a further reservation. Knowing the economic risks, we want the same level of protection for British workers as applies elsewhere in Europe.

The social model

The European social model is based on an acceptance that people have substantial rights at work. That is why European trade unions have remained stubbornly loyal to the European idea. That also explains why British trade unions led the Labour Party away from the anti-Europeanism that had dominated Labour Party thinking for a dozen years after the referendum. The more we learned about the European social model, the more we liked it. Whereas the authoritarianism of Eastern economies alienates us and the hire-and-fire mentality of North American capitalism leaves us cold, the European model, combining high levels of productivity with high levels of social protection, suits us very well. The European model makes it more difficult for companies to sack people and, if people have to lose their jobs, the European model sets a safety net sufficiently high to protect them from poverty. This prospectus was set out very clearly by Jacques Delors in his historic speech to the 1988 TUC. His message was: learn to live with the competitive pressures of a single market and the European social policy will protect you from the worst excesses of laissez-faire capitalism. That is the European project and British trade unionists have bought into it.

The social dimension of the European Union has undoubtedly delivered real benefits to working people. Successive social action programmes have strengthened moves towards equal pay, offered some protection to workers in company take-overs, improved health and safety protection, and given working people a small but increasing influence over the strategies of multi-national companies. More important still, the European Union has given trade unions a direct involvement in the design of social legislation. The process of social dialogue gives the right to the European Trade Union Confederation to make agreements with the employers' association, UNICE, which will have binding effect throughout the whole of the European Union. So far, this process has produced the Parental Leave Agreement, the Part-time Workers Agreement, and an Agreement to govern the conditions of workers on fixed term contracts. In the pipeline is the significant proposal to guarantee information and consultation rights to working people throughout Europe.

British workers have gained more than most from European social legislation. During the days of Thatcherism, British trade unions used European legislation to blunt the effect of right wing policies. The Acquired Rights Directive provided much needed protection for public service workers faced with privatisation. Equal pay legislation was used to protect part-time workers from some of the worst effects of de-regulation. The European Directive creating Works Councils in multi-national companies gave British trade unions a rare opportunity to assert some influence over strategic decisions at a time when most British companies were trying to increase the power of management. Even more beguiling was the way trade unionists were regarded. In Brussels we were consulted; in Westminster we were abused. The European social model sustained us when we needed it most.

Closing the gap

A major aim of British trade unions is to close the gap between the level of social protection available to workers in continental countries and the much lower level of social protection applying in Britain. Unfortunately, Britain's Labour Government has reservations about the European social agenda. Tony Blair consistently argues that the European labour market should be deregulated to emulate Britain's flexible labour market. The Prime Minister's attitude has surprised continental politicians. Labour was elected on a commitment to sign the Social Chapter of the European Treaties and the new government was expected to support the continuing development of social legislation. Quite the reverse. Since 1997, the Labour Government has argued against every new initiative in the Brussels social agenda. Tony Blair is even believed to have intervened personally to stiffen the opposition of British and German employers to the proposal for the European Directive on Information and Consultation.

The Government has been similarly unenthusiastic about introducing those European Directives which have been passed. The consultation document on the Working Time Directive was published six months later than planned and applied a very narrow interpretation of the new rights. The Part-time Workers Directive was introduced in a manner which limited the number of part-time workers in Britain who would benefit. The British interpretation of the Parental Leave Agreement excluded one and a half million families from its provision and it took legal action by the TUC to force the Government to change its approach.

Trade unionists want Britain to be part of the European mainstream in delivering employment rights. We certainly do not want to give our government any excuse to detach itself further. So Trade Unionists need to be careful. If we encourage the Labour Government to stay outside the single currency, Tony Blair may well argue that a British opt-out of the single currency should be accompanied by a British opt-out of social legislation.

Conditions

A less risky policy for British trade unions would be to support entry in principle and to focus debate on to those reforms which would make the eurozone and the European Union into a more congenial environment for working people. Perhaps we should be as explicit as Jacques Delors chose to be and state that we will only support entry into the single currency provided that the European Union remains committed to an expanding programme of social protection. The conditional nature of our support should be explained to the Prime Minister and to the CBI. The tendency of the employers' organisation to look at the single currency issue simply in economic terms should be relentlessly challenged.

No trade unionist would wish to rely on the market to see us through the period of insecurity and uncertainty that may follow entry into the single currency. For working people the greatest danger is that the single currency will widen the gap between the richer areas and the poorer areas of Europe. The obvious corrective is to redistribute some of Europe's extra wealth into the more disadvantaged regions by infrastructure investment, tax breaks and state subsidies. Unfortunately, these policies have become very unfashionable. In any event, the European Union does not have the resources to deliver a significant policy of redistribution. The EU budget is tiny and nearly half of that small sum is dedicated to servicing the Common Agricultural Policy. Using the European budget to redress the imbalances of wealth caused by EMU will be like trying to level the dunes of the Sahara with a single spade.

Reform

A fundamental reform of the CAP is the obvious first step towards freeing resources. The CAP costs £30 billion a year and pushes food prices way above world market levels. The CAP also mollycoddles farmers to an extent which is unthinkable elsewhere in our market economy. Whether the problem is salmonella in battery eggs, BSE in cattle or Foot and Mouth disease in livestock, the farmers are compensated when things go wrong. Fortunately, in the past year a new mood has developed in Europe to move away from subsidising farm production towards supporting stewardship of the countryside. In the single currency debate, British trade unionists should support this new thinking. We should argue that the CAP must cease to exist in its present form and that funds should be diverted into environmental support and into industrial regeneration.

After CAP reform the European Union must be persuaded to confront the budget issue head on. This involves exposing the contradictions in European political attitudes. Most commentators believe that an increase in the European budget is unthinkable because Germany in particular will not pay more. Yet Chancellor Schröder has promoted an SPD policy document in favour of stronger political union, and he gives strong support to enlargement. No-one can explain how we might achieve extensive political union in a Europe with massive differences of wealth if insufficient funds exist to reduce the gap between rich and poor. Economic and Monetary Union requires either a well funded policy designed to encourage social cohesion, or it means allowing Member States to develop such differences in wealth that joint action becomes an impossible dream. The European trade union movement should lead the campaign for a much larger European budget.

Training

And what about the aspiration of working people for more interesting jobs? The most satisfying work comes from the exercise of high quality skills. So Europe's future spending plans must give a higher priority to education and training. Amongst industrialised nations, Britain has a poor record of training in general and an appalling level of illiteracy and innumeracy. However, we should not believe the propaganda that the French and the Germans provide adequate role models. When the European Commission carried out a survey to establish the extent of in-work training throughout the European Union, it revealed that most European Union countries are not much better than Britain in providing vocational training for existing employees.

Even if we take a very generous view of the training element in various European initiatives, the GMB estimates that well under 2 per cent of the European budget is spent on training or training related activities. This is less than the European Union spends on pig meat and a good deal less than it spends on agricultural set-aside. Since the Lisbon Summit, almost every statement from the European Council or from the European Commission tells the people of Europe that increased employability must be the aim of public policy. To the shame of the European Union, these sentiments have never been matched by an adequate level of investment. Increased spending on education and training must be a key trade union demand in every debate about the future of the European Union.

Priorities

Sceptics on the left may argue that a policy of conditional support for a single currency is no more than a convenient fudge. Of course, conditional support is always a difficult stance to maintain. The risk is that conditions will be stripped away until all that remains is a stark position of support inadequately covered by a few words of threadbare rhetoric. Indeed, the formidable programme put forward in this chapter - social protection, reform of the CAP, budget enlargement, redistribution in favour of poorer areas, and a major increase in training expenditure - invites the criticism that it is too ambitious to be taken seriously.

So priorities have to be established. In the first place, trade union support for the single currency should be fully conditional on the EU's continued commitment to the European Social Model. If the politicians of Europe have nothing to offer working people but an unregulated labour market with rising insecurity and ever more powerful employers, trade union support for the single currency must be forfeit because there will be no benefit to justify the risk. Second, trade unionists must insist on much higher spending on training because low skills will condemn working people to insecure, low quality and monotonous jobs. As for the other conditions, miracles are not on the agenda, but we need a European budget which is growing rapidly enough to fund substantial regional support.

This programme cannot be achieved by trade unionists acting alone. Success in the European Union of the future will increasingly depend on making effective alliances. Given the nature of the programme, it is likely that allies will be found more easily on the continent than in Britain and more easily in the European Parliament than in the Council of Ministers. That is the nature of the new politics of Europe. Fortunately, the trade union movement is more prepared for that challenge than almost any other institution in Britain.

Chapter 10

Keep the Pound 'for the Foreseeable Future'

by Ruth Lea

Editor's Commentary

Although the thrust of the majority of contributions to this book is political, the economic arguments cannot be ignored. There is a cynical view that the Chancellor's five tests can be deemed to have been met (or not) when the Government so decides, although the Prime Minister has repeatedly stressed his conviction that the economic judgment must be favourable. For the majority of members of the Institute of Directors the economic judgment is negative, in contrast to the views of most of the biggest industrialists in the country.

*The IoD view, clearly articulated by **Ruth Lea**, puts the economic arguments first. She is not convinced that there has been sufficient sustainable convergence between Britain and the countries in the Eurozone to make a success of membership of the single currency. The political arguments do not weigh as heavily with her, since she fears the UK is likely to remain a minority voice in or out. It follows that for her the few disadvantages of staying out fade into insignificance compared with the risks of premature membership.*

Keep the pound 'for the foreseeable future'

by Ruth Lea

Introduction

One of the key requirements for business to thrive is macroeconomic stability. The experience of the 'booms and busts' of the 1960s, 1970s, 1980s and early 1990s are remembered only too well by businesspeople as they endeavoured to cope with roller-coaster interest rates and, especially in the mid 1970s, rocketing inflation rates. And, even though we were not reduced to using wheelbarrows for carrying notes when going shopping during this period, I remember the difficulties of annualised double-digit inflation only too well.

Since our ignoble eviction from the Exchange Rate Mechanism (ERM) by the foreign exchange markets on 16 September 1992 (a date etched on my heart), the British economy has performed well in terms of macroeconomic stability and certainly much better than in the previous thirty years. The Monetary Policy Committee (MPC) of the Bank of England (BoE) is serving the British economy well and the prospect of presenting its members with P45s (figurative, you understand) and replacing them with the European Central Bank (ECB) fills me with foreboding. As a nation we suffered for many years with economic instability and the notion that we might risk our new-style stability (which had been the economic equivalent of the Holy Grail for decades) for a political integrationist project I find deeply concerning.

And, yes, of course, Economic and Monetary Union (EMU) is a political project. As the Rome Treaty made crystal clear ('the ever closer union of the people's of Europe') the European movement is one of increasing political integration. Few decisions could have such wide-ranging implications as handing over the control of your economy to federal institutions and replacing your notes and coins (symbols of nationhood) with the Euro. But this article is about the economics of replacing the pound with the Euro – not about politics or images of nationhood.

The need for appropriate interest rates

The key to macroeconomic, low inflation stability is, of course, a satisfactory mix of fiscal and monetary policies. For many years the UK Government's broad policy strategy (irrespective of party) has been to concentrate on monetary policy for fine-tuning the economy, given the overall fiscal policy stance. This seems eminently sensible but it does place an enormous responsibility on the monetary authorities to make the correct decisions concerning the appropriate level of interest rates. It puts the need for appropriate interest rates centre stage of the management of the economy. And if you transfer the setting of interest rates from the BoE to the ECB you are, de facto, transferring the major tool of economic management from a national institution that only has to consider national circumstances (albeit complicated by the regional dimension) to an international institution which has to consider many economies with all their national and regional disparities.

The consequences of the inappropriate level of interest rates are all too painful to remember. May I take the last two instances. In the late 1980s Chancellor Lawson was shadowing the DM (prior to intended ERM entry) at DM3 to the pound. The markets treated this target as target practice and repeatedly pushed the pound above this level (despite considerable BoE intervention). Lawson cut rates and by mid-1988 they were down to 7 per cent - even though the housing market was red-hot. The UK experienced an inflationary boom. Interest rates had been too low for domestic circumstances.

The opposite occurred in the early 1990s. The UK economy had already gone into recession by the time the UK joined the ERM in October 1990 as the aggressive interest rate increases intended to control the Lawson boom took effect. But the recession was undoubtedly extended by membership of the ERM and the need to maintain interest rates at least a tad above German rates in order to hold the pound within its ERM bands. German rates had soared to nearly 10 per cent in the wake of German unification as the Bundesbank sought to control the subsequent inflationary boom. On the eve of 16 September 1992 UK rates were 10 per cent. These rates were clearly far too high for domestic circumstances and had viciously contributed to the prolonging of the recession. (And, incidentally, were down to 6 per cent by the end of January 1993.)

So inappropriate interest rates lead to 'boom and bust.' And handing the determination of interest rate for the British economy to the ECB, with its 'one size fits all' rates, seriously risks a return to instability.

Cyclical convergence

For the UK to adopt the ECB's interest rates without a return to boom and bust, there must be, as a very minimum, cyclical convergence. Of course, there has undoubtedly been some 'convergence' of growth rates and unemployment rates as 'core' euroland has caught up cyclically with the British economy over the last 2-3 years. But, ironically, some of this cyclical convergence has occurred because the UK has had higher interest rates than euroland since the Euro was launched at the start of 1999. If the UK had joined the Euro at launch then the economy would probably be now experiencing an inflationary boom as Ireland has experienced – unless there had been severe fiscal tightening. According to the OECD estimates.[1] Ireland's private consumption deflator rose by 6.5 per cent in 2000 compared with 3.3 per cent in 1999 whilst euroland's average in 2000 was 2.2 per cent. There were also considerable disparities between other euroland countries with Spanish and Finnish consumer inflation rates were well above the average whilst French and German rates were below. So far this year (to June) Ireland's rate has slipped back – but major disparities between countries remain.

 But, even with the 'convergence' seen so far, there are arguably still significant differences in 'output gaps'[2] and unemployment rates (two measures of capacity utilisation and hence 'cyclical convergence') between euroland and the UK that still require interest rates to be higher in Britain. The OECD[3] estimates that the 'output gap' for euroland was still negative in 2000 (in other words the economy still showed some slack) whereas the UK's gap was positive. Turning to unemployment rates, euroland's unemployment rate was 9.0 per cent[4] in 2000 compared with the UK's 5.5 per cent. (As with inflation rates, there were significant disparities between euroland economies for both output gaps and unemployment.)

Now, even though both these measures of cyclical convergence are open to criticism, for this writer, writing in June 2001, the case that Britain has cyclically converged, even on a temporary basis, has yet to be robustly made.

Sustainable convergence

But even if the juggernaut of the British economy could be synchronised cyclically with euroland, the key question would then be would such convergence be sustainable – or would the convergence merely be a matter of 'ships passing in the night' as the current BoE Governor has hinted at.[5]   And the key to sustainable convergence with euroland is whether the British economy is sufficiently similar structurally to cope with the 'one size fits all' interest rate policy. The need for structural compatibility is twofold. Firstly, economies within a common currency area should react to external shocks (eg the tripling of oil prices) in a similar way ('symmetric' as opposed to 'asymmetric' shocks) so the direction of the monetary policy response to the shocks is appropriate for all.   And, secondly, when interest rates are changed then the 'transmission mechanism' between interest rate changes and the impact on the real economy is similar for all.

Many analysts have pointed out the structural differences between the UK and the rest of the EU including HM Treasury:[6]

> 'No two countries are ever identical but the UK has certain features that clearly make it different from other countries in the EU.'

And the Treasury went on to point out some very fundamental differences between the UK and core euroland. Concerning the risk of 'asymmetric shocks' the Treasury pointed out Britain's role as an oil producer and, arguably more significantly, the different trade patterns. Concerning the latter, the US, for example, accounts for 17 per cent of the UK's current account credits compared with only 9 per cent for the EU 14 (ie the EU excluding the UK) and 10 per cent individually for Germany, France and Italy.[7]   Conversely, the UK's trade with the EU was under 50 per cent compared with 65 per cent for the EU 14 and 56 per cent, 60 per cent and 59 per cent for Germany, France and Italy respectively. It is clear, therefore, that the UK is much more influenced by US trade than are the other EU countries and therefore, along with the significance of US inward investment, Britain's economic fortunes are more tied up with the US.

Turning to the transmission mechanism, the Treasury strongly implied that Britain was more susceptible to changes in short-term interest rates than her major EU partners.[8] The increased sensitivity reflected a combination of high owner occupation and a high stock of mortgage debt at variable rates. We would add that, even though there has been a modest move towards fixed-rate mortgages in recent years, the annual data are volatile and the trends are not unambiguous.[9]

In addition to the Treasury's concerns we would add the importance of convergence in the structural unemployment rate or NAIRU (non-accelerating inflation rate of unemployment) for 'sustainable convergence.' If countries were not 'NAIRU converged' then inflationary pressures would arise earlier in countries with the higher NAIRUs and require a tighter policy response than in countries with the lower NAIRUs (other things being equal). Evidence suggests that the UK's NAIRU is significantly lower than for, say, Germany.[10]

In conclusion, the hundred-dollar question isn't just a matter of cyclical convergence; it is crucially a matter of when structural differences will be so insignificant that sustainable convergence will be possible. I do not pretend to know the answer and I do not know anyone who does know the answer. But without an answer we should not even contemplate giving up the pound and adopting the Euro 'for the foreseeable future.' It would be pure folly.

The Maastricht criteria and the 'Five Economic Tests'

The five Maastricht criteria[11] were originally agreed at the Maastricht summit (December 1991) for eligibility for the Euro and covered inflation, long-term interest rates, the Government debt/GDP ratio (which was fairly spectacularly 'overlooked' in the case of Belgium, Italy and Greece), the Government deficit/GDP ratio, and exchange rate stability (in other words staying within ERM narrow bands for two years). With the exception of ERM membership Britain passes the Maastricht criteria with flying colours. But we do not, of course, believe that the Maastricht criteria are any way nearly exacting enough. They barely touch on cyclical convergence and they most certainly don't tackle sustainable convergence.

The Treasury's 'Five Economic Tests'[12] are altogether of a different order of sophistication – though they are qualitative rather than quantitative which leaves them open to 'political' interpretation.[13] Moreover, the Treasury made it very clear that 'sustainable and durable convergence is the touchstone [of membership] and without it we cannot reap the benefits of a successful EMU.' Such convergence meant 'that the UK economy was sufficiently and durably converged with the other members' economies to make participation permanently viable and that the UK economy was sufficiently flexible to respond to shocks and other changes that will occur over time.'

The tests were:

Convergence (the key criterion): are business cycles and economic structures compatible so that we and others could live comfortably with Euro interest rates on a permanent basis?

Flexibility: if problems emerge is there sufficient flexibility (in both the product and labour markets)?

Investment: would joining EMU create better conditions for firms making long-term decisions about the UK?

Financial services: what impact would entry into EMU have on the competitive position of the UK's financial services industry, particularly the City's wholesale markets?

Employment and growth: in summary, will joining EMU promote higher growth, stability and a lasting increase in jobs?

And the Treasury's conclusions were remarkably downbeat.

Briefly, they were:

Convergence: the British economy was not cyclically converged and, as we have already discussed, the structural differences (including trade patterns, oil, company finance and the housing market) were important not simply because they made the UK susceptible to different types of shocks, but also because they affected how the UK responded to the shocks via the transmission mechanism.

Flexibility: in the labour market, in particular, the UK had not yet achieved sufficient flexibility. Concerning wage flexibility it was not clear that enough had been achieved for successful EMU membership (ie wages were too rigid) and labour mobility was low compared with, say, the US.[14]

Investment: investment would be damaged if we entered EMU before durable and flexible convergence (which had not been achieved).

Financial services: early EMU membership should be positive.

Employment and growth: benefits would only accrue if there were sufficient convergence and flexibility.

The Treasury's analysis was undertaken in 1997 but we believe that their conclusions are just as valid today as they were then. Indeed, given the increased employment regulations, the underlying situation has probably deteriorated.

We would add the following comments:

Convergence: as we have already discussed we do not believe that we have cyclically converged yet even though there have been some superficial 'progress' since 1997. There has been little 'progress' on the structural differences.

Flexibility: Britain's labour market has become more inflexible since 1997 because of the introduction of extra employment regulations including the minimum wage, increased collective and individual rights, 'family friendly' regulations, Social Chapter Directives and the working time regulations.[15] If the UK were to join the Euro, experience inappropriately high interest rates and suffer from recession (as in the ERM between 1990 and 1992), it is highly unlikely that wages would be sufficiently flexible to prevent the labour market adjustment primarily working through employment and resulting in higher unemployment.

Investment: on the specific issue of inward investment, and despite apocalyptic warnings if we did not enter the Euro, inward investment was at record levels last year.

Financial services: there are no signs that the City is suffering from being outside euroland. On the contrary, being an 'offshore island' without vested interests in the main currency of a geographical area (Europe in this case) is probably helpful for international financial centres.

Employment and growth: there is little to add to the Treasury's analysis. Benefits would only accrue if there is sufficient convergence and flexibility and costs will accrue if we join the Euro prematurely and return to the bad old days of 'boom and bust.'

Exchange rate issues

When potential UK membership of the Euro is discussed by euroenthusiasts there is much talk about the need for 'stable' exchange rates and an end to 'uncertainty,' with this type of stability being seen as the 'external' equivalent of 'internal' stability of low inflation macroeconomic stability. Moreover, membership of the Euro would mean there was more price 'transparency' (though trading firms are well acquainted multiple currencies and multiple price lists) and savings would be made on transactions costs (though possibly only 0.1 per cent to 0.2 per cent of GDP).

Even though there is some intuitive appeal for such exchange rate 'stability' the following points should be borne in mind:

Some of the richest countries in the world are also some of the smallest currency areas (for example, Singapore, Switzerland and Norway). This suggests that exchange rate uncertainty is not a big obstacle to economic efficiency. Moreover, Canada has kept its dollar despite being more integrated with the US than the UK is with the EU. And, incidentally, Switzerland is more economically integrated with the EU than the UK is and yet in March 2001 nearly 77 per cent of the Swiss voted against closer political integration with the EU;

If the UK joined the Euro, then the relationship of its currency to the Euro bloc wouldn't be so much one of 'stability' as 'rigor mortis' and any possible exchange rate 'flexibility' within the bloc (which can be a useful tool of macroeconomic management) would be permanently ruled out. Moreover, if the historically high $/Euro volatility were to persist, then volatility with the $ would increase for the UK;

According to HM Customs and Excise[16] a high proportion of the UK's visible trade is invoiced in dollars. 27 per cent of exports were invoiced in dollars in 1999 - along with 52 per cent in sterling, 12 per cent in Euros (and legacy currencies) and 9 per cent in other currencies. 30 per cent of imports were invoiced in dollars - along with 40 per cent in sterling, 14 per cent in Euros and 16 per cent in other currencies. If the UK joined the Euro, it is likely that a fairly high proportion of UK trade would continue to be invoiced in dollars and would suffer from the higher $ volatility discussed in the previous point;

As we have already discussed premature membership of the Euro risks damaging internal stability. This is not a price worth paying for external 'stability' when only 15 per cent of GDP (strictly, of total final expenditure) is traded with euroland (only 50 per cent of our external trade is with euroland);

If the UK joined the Euro, there would be some benefits for businesses trading with euroland but it is worth bearing in mind the very considerable costs of conversion (and, of course, every business would be affected). Accountants Chantry Vellacott estimate that the total conversion costs would be £36bn (3 per cent of GDP);

Last but by no means least, is the thorny issue of the exchange rate level at possible entry. Since its launch, the Euro has been surprisingly weak against the pound and this has undoubtedly hindered British exporters. The preferred entry rate for IoD members[17] is around DM2.75 (1.4 Euros). At the time of writing (June 2001) the sterling exchange rate is around 1.6 Euros implying that business would like to see a devaluation of the pound against the Euro of well over 10 per cent. To enter at a rate of around 1.6 Euros to the pound would be to lock Britain into an uncompetitive rate permanently.

The role of fiscal policy

Under the discussion of the Treasury's Five Economic Tests we touched on possible remedies for dealing with an economy locked in EMU, with inappropriately high interest rates and in recession. We concluded that there would not be the necessary wage flexibility to prevent higher unemployment (a situation which would be exacerbated by low EU labour mobility).

Clearly an economy in such a situation could not resort to cutting interest rates or devaluing the currency. One alternative, therefore, would be expansionary fiscal policy. But the scope for countries to expand fiscally could be very constrained by the Stability and Growth Pact which, elaborating on the Maastricht Treaty's fiscal rules, sets a 3 per cent of GDP limit on budget deficits, though with an escape clause for modest temporary overshoots due to exceptional circumstances such as a severe recession. The scope for national Governments to act would, therefore, be very limited.

Moreover, there would be, on current EU policies, very little help by way of fiscal transfers from Brussels. The EU federal budget cannot be more than 1.27 per cent of EU GDP, which compares with the US federal budget of nearly 20 per cent of GDP. (This is one reason why comparisons between euroland and the US are unconvincing - along with the relative lack of labour market flexibility and labour market mobility in the EU.)

The relative smallness of the federal budget led the MacDougall Report[18] to argue for centralised tax and transfer arrangements in Europe similar to those in other federations; it estimated that an expansion of the EU budget to around 5-7 per cent of community-wide GDP would be desirable. But, as yet, the MacDougall Report has not been acted on (and we do not wish to see it acted on).

Loss of influence in the EU

Hardly a week goes by without an EU official (including Commission President Romano Prodi) claiming that the UK will lose influence if we don't join the Euro.

Well, the UK is a fully paid up member of the EU (and how - given our budget contributions!) and our voice in EU-wide matters should be, without question, as influential (or not as the case might be) out of the Euro as in. On taxes, for example, we retain our veto and the current Chancellor has successfully resisted the imposition of the withholding tax. On other matters, such as turning the EU into 'the most dynamic and competitive knowledge-based economy in the world by 2010' by liberalising various product markets (an agenda for which was developed during last year's Portuguese presidency), the UK is likely to remain a minority voice whether we are in the Euro or out. The British way of 'doing things' is quite simply a minority way of 'doing things' in the EU – whatever our currency. And I cannot understand why British politicians ever think that this will change.

When it comes to economic management of euroland then clearly we cannot expect to have much influence. After all, euroland has little influence over the way we manage our macro-economy.

A final thought. Every so often blood curdling 'horror' stories hit the British press such as '3 million jobs lost' if we don't join the Euro. The 'analysis' behind this curious statement is that jobs relying on our exports to Euroland will be 'lost' if we don't join the Euro, because the rest of the EU will be viciously protectionist and stop buying our goods. Well, such behaviour would break every rule in the EU and WTO trading book and, as we have a visible trade deficit with the rest of the EU, would not even be in our EU partners' trading interests. There is also the curious assumption that we would not 'find' the jobs currently 'lost' by imports from the EU if we were to stop trading with the EU.

Conclusions

As an economist I have studied the balance sheet for Britain's membership of the Euro and I am convinced that Britain should not join the Euro 'for the foreseeable future.' Moreover, a majority of our members support this view.[19] When we surveyed our members in 1999, the proportion of respondents saying Britain should not join the Euro 'in the foreseeable future' or the stronger 'should never join' totalled 55 per cent. 43 per cent said either 'as soon as possible' or 'in the foreseeable future (5 years).' (We were keen to ask our members practical questions about actual membership and not hypothetical questions about whether they were in favour of Euro membership 'in principle.')

There are a few disadvantages for keeping the pound (including transactions costs). But these fade into insignificance compared with the risks of premature membership of the Euro. Premature membership risks throwing away our hard won macro-economic stability – a stability so lacking for most of the 1960s, 1970s, 1980s and the early 1990s. 'If it ain't broke, don't fix it!'

Notes

[1] OECD: *Economic outlook* (OECD, December 2000). Consumer prices inflation as measured by the Harmonised Index of Consumer Prices (HICP) shows a similar pattern. According to the ONS: *Consumer price indices: March 2001* (ONS, 19 April 2001), Ireland's HICP inflation touched 6 per cent in the 2nd half of 2000.

[2] Output gaps are defined as 'deviations of actual GDP from potential GDP as a percentage of potential GDP.' Output gaps are a measure of capacity utilisation. A 'positive output gap' suggests that an economy has been growing too fast, pointing to renewed inflationary pressures; a negative gap is a sign of slack.

[3] OECD: *Economic outlook* (OECD, December 2000).

[4] Unemployment rates are 'commonly used definitions.' The source is OECD: *Economic outlook* (OECD, December 2000).

[5] And see Leach: *The UK and Euroland – ships passing in the night* (IoD, September 2000).

[6] HM Treasury: *UK membership of the single currency: an assessment of the five economic tests* (HM Treasury, October 1997).

[7] Eurostat: *Geographical breakdown of the EU current account 1995-98* (Eurostat, 2000). Please note that the recorded UK export data overstate the amount of exports going to the EU, and understate the amount going outside the EU, because of the Rotterdam-Antwerp Effect and the separate Netherlands Distortion. It is likely therefore that the real divergence in trade patterns between the UK and the rest of the EU is more pronounced than quoted in the text. The data are 1998 data.

[8] In addition the econometric evidence, on the whole, supports the conclusion that the British economy is more short-term interest-rate sensitive than say, the French or German economies. See OECD: *EMU, facts, challenges and policies* (OECD, 1999) which concluded that single country macro models and the Fed MCM multi-country macro model (used by the BIS) clearly confirmed Britain's interest rate sensitivity. Leach: *The UK and the Euro – better out than in?* (IoD, April 1999) quoted Maclennan, Muellbauer & Stephens (OREP, Autumn 1998) who argued that 'simulations with large macro-models show large interest rate effects on output in the UK, consistent with these findings predicted by economic reasoning. The fact that research using VAR (vector auto regressive) methodology has arrived at less conclusive results has persuaded some economists that these are minor issues. However...research using VARs is seriously flawed.' Leach also said that the European Commission had highlighted the limitations of VAR and their dubious conclusions (in *Economic Policy in EMU – a study by the European Commission*, OUP 1998).

[9] According to the Council for Mortgage Lenders (CML), the per cent of 'new' mortgages at fixed rates was 50 per cent in 1994 - but dropped to 20 per cent in 1996. The per cent rose to 55 per cent in 1998 and then fell to 34 per cent in 2000. The per cent of the outstanding book (by value) which was fixed rate was 21 per cent in 1994, falling to 19 per cent in 1997 and then rising to 27 per cent in 1999.

[10] Leach: *The UK and Euroland – ships passing in the night* (IoD, September 2000).

[11] The five Maastricht criteria were: (1) inflation (measured by CPI) must have been within 1.5 per cent of the EC's 3 best performers over the period of a year; (2) long-term interest rates must have been within 2 per cent of the EC's 3 best performers over the period of a year; (3) the Government sector debt/GDP ratio should be no more than 60 per cent; (4) the Government deficit/GDP ratio should be no more than 3 per cent and (5) currencies should have been kept within the narrow ERM bands, for at least 2 years.

[12] HM Treasury: *UK membership of the single currency: an assessment of the five economic tests* (HM Treasury, October 1997). Davies: *Assessing EMU: two cheers for the Treasury* (IoD, November 1997) was the IoD's largely favourable response to the Five Tests.

[13] Leach: *The UK and Euroland – ships passing in the night* (IoD, September 2000) included an IoD Convergence Contract which specific quantitative targets. The Contract was 'adopted' by *The Sun*!

[14] For further relevant comments on labour mobility see also (1) Currie: *The pros and cons of EMU* (HM Treasury, July 1997) and (2) OECD: *EMU, facts, challenges and policies* (OECD, 1999).

[15] Lea: *The Work-Life Balance...and all that: the re-regulation of the labour market* (IoD, April 2001).

[16] HM Customs and Excise: *UK imports and exports: currency of invoicing* (ONS/C&E press release, 23 February 2001).

[17] Lea: *UK membership of the Euro* (IoD, June 1999).

[18] European Commission: *Report of the study group on the role of public finance in European integration* (MacDougall report) (European Commission, 1977).

[19] Lea: *UK membership of the Euro* (IoD, June 1999).

Chapter 11

The Euro and London

by Ken Livingstone

Editor's Commentary

Many of those who favour joining the Euro do so out of concern for the position of the City of London as the financial capital of Europe. Noting that failure to join so far has not affected either this situation or inward investment, many sceptics are unconvinced by the argument. For me, however, it is fascinating how quickly **Ken Livingstone,** *not a traditional supporter of Britain in Europe, has as the newly elected Mayor of London become convinced of the need for sterling to join the single currency. True, he does not believe it would guarantee London's position, but outside it would be impossible to sustain it in the medium term. The collapse of the Bretton Woods system requires a single European currency, and London's interests require Britain to be in it.*

The Euro and London

by Ken Livingstone

As Mayor of London it is part of my duty and responsibility to help ensure that London remains the financial centre of Europe. A decision in the referendum for sterling to join the single currency would not, of course, by itself be sufficient to maintain London's position; but to be blunt: a decision which led to Britain staying outside the Euro would be incompatible in the long run with retaining London's pre-eminence as the financial capital of Europe.

Globalisation

Some argue that globalisation makes the single currency, and the question of Britain's membership of it – of secondary importance – if not irrelevant. Look, they say, London has not suffered since the inception of the Euro. Perhaps, but it would be folly to assume that could continue. It may be true that today, in expertise, critical mass of companies, weight in world markets and business infrastructure, London considerably outclasses any other European city as a financial centre and is enjoying great prosperity. But the competition which London is now facing in the financial global market place presents a challenge which cannot be properly met outside one of the world's great currency areas. Already London's competitive position has been weakened by well-publicised problems in investment banking, and the necessary reorganisation in the futures and derivatives market.

The prospects for the stock exchange are uncertain. Many present and potential investors are waiting for a decision on the Euro.

It is true that London does offer many advantages as an international city and already brings strength to Europe, but it is vital to exploit its full scope. The fact that London is Europe's financial capital, when the UK is far from being Europe's largest economy, is due to the internationalisation of the city. The vast diversity of London is ultimately rooted in that and it would be foolhardy to assume that the attraction of the investment and skilled labour necessary to maintain London's position is compatible with a narrow-minded Little Englander approach. Globalisation inevitably gives greater weight to a country's capital as the main gateway to its economy, and as I have often pointed out, many international companies will only either invest in London or not come to Britain. Furthermore, the UK domestic economy is much less important for British firms than is the US domestic economy for American firms, so that London's prosperity is inseparably connected to its role in the international economy. It must tap all the opportunities and not impose a sort of mini-balkanisation on itself.

Optimal scale

While modern production and investment have outgrown the scale of individual European states, including that of the UK, it has not yet reached an unlimited size. This might happen before the end of this century, but today there is clear empirical evidence that the three major blocs of the world economy – the US, Japan and the European Union – may represent the optimal size of economic unit for the beginning of the 21st century. They are certainly strikingly similar in their fundamental economic dimensions both in terms of GDP and the proportion of GDP accounted for by international trade. Having found the optimal scale, it makes no sense to fail to take full advantage of it by ignoring its logic.

Many arguments against membership of the Euro are, in fact, arguments against membership of the European Union itself. Those who oppose joining the Euro pretend that they favour membership of a trading bloc but not further forms of integration, particularly a common currency. But this is rather like wanting to swim without getting wet. For a market, not excluding the EU single market, to be effective it needs a level playing field on which all participants are bound by the same rules. An effective integrated and competitive market cannot exist if the elimination of tariffs is accompanied by different standards and subsidies.

The elimination of tariffs was the key factor in the formation of the EEC, as a Common Market, because it took place at a time of fixed exchange rates under the Bretton Woods system. As long as these existed (with an allowance for periodic adjustments) the elimination of tariffs and standardisation of conditions for the members were sufficient to maintain an open and stable market. But once the Bretton Woods system collapsed, and universal fixed exchange rates ceased to exist (particularly between EU members), Europe was necessarily driven towards a single currency. It did not need one as long as all exchange rates were fixed, but once that situation no longer existed, a single currency was required in order to maintain the stability of the market. A 15 per cent devaluation is just as effective as a 15 per cent tariff.

London's two economies

Now the Euro is there, and can be seen to have been inevitable. It will not go away. We now have to consider the effect on our country of remaining outside, and I as Mayor need to take account of London's specific interests. They are not different from those of the UK as a whole, but highlight in a more acute form the wider concerns.

London is unique in the UK, indeed in Europe, in that it has in a sense two economies, each governed by somewhat different dynamics. The first is driven by the UK business cycle. Its dynamics are determined by the normal considerations of interest and exchange rates and so on. The problems faced by manufacturing in London, for example, are essentially those faced in the country as a whole. London's second economy, that of the City of London, is more tightly integrated into the global economy and is more directly driven by international factors. For the City, developments such as movements in East Asian currencies or a default on Russian Treasury bonds are at least as potent as upheavals in the domestic economy. London can only prosper when both parts of its economy thrive. The Euro is of decisive importance because membership is the only means of knitting together both sectors of London's economy to ensure the city's prosperity.

Maintaining London's position

I mentioned earlier the three key currency blocs which have emerged in the global economy. Each will have a financial centre: as in every other sphere size and concentration are critical factors. At the moment London is, clearly and by several times, the dominant financial centre in Europe. Given this advantage I have never suggested that if Britain does not join the Euro the City will lose its position immediately: but in the medium term there can be little doubt about the outcome. Only entry into the single currency can secure for the City of London the continuation of its present advantages and its position in Europe for at least the next half century. Not only will it still dominate the continent's finance but will continue to attract the great US and Japanese financial institutions looking to do business in the eurozone – not to mention the Europeans.

It is equally clear that Europe will not allow its currency to be controlled via a financial centre in a country which is not a member of the Euro. Nor is there any force strong enough to compel it to do so. If through Britain's decision in the referendum London in effect decides that it does not want to be, or does no care if it is or is not, the financial centre of the new Euro-dominated Europe, then Euroland will build its own financial and monetary centre. The only question is whether it will be in Frankfurt or Berlin. It may take a decade or more, but the City of London will have effectively and decisively marginalized itself. I have already referred to setbacks in the City's dominance of the financial field: if Britain remains outside the single currency these setbacks are likely to become more frequent, more generalised and more persistent.

Consider for a moment the position of the City of London, outside the Euro, from a different angle. There is no place in the new world economy for a sterling bloc, just as there is no place for an isolated UK economy in the world. Outside the eurozone London would, in reality, be competing with New York within a single dollar bloc. There is no doubting that the outcome of such a struggle would not see London as the victor.

Campaigning for London

The Chancellor of the Exchequer has set the Government's five economic criteria for Euro membership, but from London's point of view the reasons for joining the single currency are even more fundamental. It is the only way to be sure that London's productive economy competes effectively in its largest market – Europe, and, I repeat, the only way over the medium term for the City of London to remain Europe's financial capital. Without that, there will be no long term. Precisely because of the dual character of its economy, to which I referred above, London has an even greater interest in British membership than the rest of the country. That is why, of course, business support joining the Euro is even stronger in London than in other parts of the UK. It is also the reason why, before and since becoming Mayor I have campaigned in favour of membership.

I understand the reasons, though I regret the result, why the Government's campaign in favour was until the election tactically paralysed, but considerations which might have applied at a national level are not necessarily valid in London. Therefore London's campaign should be based on an assumption that the government's five criteria will be fulfilled and followed by the launch of a full-hearted campaign actively led by the Prime Minister. Second, national tactical considerations should no longer prevent London from arguing most effectively in our own way for Euro membership. We must involve all those who support membership. It may not be the issue which takes up the largest part of the Mayor's time on a day-to-day basis, but from the point of view of the medium and longer-term future of London it is the most important strategic issue confronting the city. And we are unlikely to be able to correct the adverse effects of the wrong decision.

Chapter 12

Not as Things Stand

by Janet Bush

Editor's Commentary

New Europe is one of the more interesting organisations campaigning against joining the Euro, because unlike some others it is not hostile to British membership of the EU as such. **Janet Bush** *has said she has tried hard to listen to the arguments in favour of the further step which the euro would represent but is not convinced by them. She accepts that the price of losing political independence involved in joining might be worth paying if the economic arguments were decisively in favour; or that if the political prize were overwhelmingly positive, even bad economics could be dealt with. But having looked at the arguments she remains of the view that both the politics and economics look risky and unappealing, while saying 'No' would cause no damage.*

Not as things stand

by Janet Bush

Great tribal passions are aroused by the question of whether Britain should join the Euro or not. For those who advocate membership, on this decision hangs Britain's European destiny, the chance to demonstrate that Britain really is at the heart of Europe and a golden land of economic opportunity. For EMU-sceptics, the Euro is a monumental economic gamble and a Rubicon that must not be crossed if Britain is to remain an independent democracy. Anyone who thinks that the Euro is a question of avoiding commission fees at Thomas Cook is missing the point entirely.

Emotions will dominate the referendum campaign. But perhaps a cool-headed cost benefit analysis might be more useful. My view is that if the economic arguments were decisively in favour of joining the Euro – and this is the Government's overriding test – then the loss of political independence that joining Economic and Monetary Union entails might be a price worth paying. If the political prize were overwhelmingly positive, then even bad economics could be dealt with. If both the economics and politics of EMU look risky and unappetising, then the case for joining falls apart.

I believe that the economics of EMU make no sense for Britain and is risky for others. The main problem – which manifested itself dramatically in Britain during sterling's brief sojourn in the Exchange Rate Mechanism – is that it is exceedingly difficult for a very large economic area to live comfortably with a single interest rate.

The theory, before the launch of the Euro, was that economies would comply with the convergence criteria of the Maastricht Treaty and thereby be aligned permanently enough to be able to live with a single interest rate. This theory is deeply flawed. Firstly, the criteria are strictly macroeconomic. They do not take into account the much more complex behaviours/characteristics of different economies. For example, one economy may be far more susceptible to an oil shock than another. One may have more 'flexible' labour markets than another. Secondly, there was a great deal of fudging of the criteria in order to make sure that a large number of economies complied and could launch the Euro. Thirdly, convergence is not permanent. Economies are dynamic. The 'snapshot' of apparent convergence on January 1 1999 has already changed dramatically. Significant divergence has appeared since the Euro was launched, even in relatively benign economic circumstances. The economic stewards of euroland must have their fingers firmly crossed as they wait to see how the component economies of the eurozone fare if the economic slowdown in America turns into something close to recession.

Ireland was, and is, the best case study of how a single European interest rate can cause trouble. Ireland's inflation rate is far above the euroland average, largely because Ireland's interest rates had to be halved when it swapped Irish rates for a Euro rate at the launch of the Euro which poured oil on the flames of an already robust economic expansion. And there was nothing, as the ECB said, that could be done. The Euro interest is set for the aggregate interests of the 11 countries of the eurozone and Ireland's needs happen not to have suited the single interest rate prevailing over the past two years. Ireland has, in short, a problem of economic success in the midst of economic mediocrity.

The solution proposed for Ireland by the Commission and European finance ministers was – with no monetary get-out – fiscal. This is why Ireland was formally reprimanded at a meeting of European finance ministers in February for its plans to cut taxes – justified, for domestic reasons, on the grounds of, inter alia, a budget surplus of 4.7 per cent of Irish GDP, the best in the EU.

The EU takes a view, of course, not of Ireland's domestic priorities but of the eurozone's as a whole: Ireland's tax cuts would - whatever their national justification - destabilise euroland (despite the fact that Ireland accounts for only 1 per cent of euroland GDP). So, for the first time in the Euro's short history, there was a conflict between a eurozone member's domestic interests and that of the eurozone as a whole.

The Irish case also throws up another key debate about how the eurozone should be run. What role should fiscal policy play? There are two models that probably have to run in parallel to sustain monetary union in the long term: fiscal flexibility and competition on one hand and fiscal centralisation on the other.

There is a strong argument that fiscal policy – taxes and public spending – has to be more flexible to build room for manoeuvre into a single monetary system. America has some of this fiscal flexibility at state level and there is a conviction among economists that not only does this loosen the rigidities of a monetary union at the margin but that it also makes a single market more dynamic.

But running in parallel with the flexibility at state level in the US is a large measure of centralisation into a single federal budget which provides the real oil to lubricate monetary union – fiscal transfers. In America, between 19 per cent and 25 per cent of the huge US federal budget is available to distribute taxpayers' money to regions that are hit when monetary policy or other developments turn against them. So, a Californian property bust can be bailed out by money paid into a central pool by other states.

So America has marginal tax flexibility at state level and enormous flexibility at federal level through the ability to transfer money to those regions or states that might temporarily be at the wrong end of overall monetary policy.

How does Europe compare with this? The answer is that Europe is in a terrible muddle and the reason for the muddle is that, very unusually, monetary union has preceded political union. Usually, monetary unions come into being because a political union has been formed and as Otmar Issing, chief economist at the European Central Bank has famously said: 'There is no example in history of a lasting monetary union without a single state.' Monetary unions usually break down when political unions break down – witness the Czech Republic and Slovakia in recent times.

The lack of political solidarity (union) means that euroland is unable to 'do the right thing fiscally.' In the single market, it should have tax flexibility at state level to provide the necessary competition and dynamism. This is difficult without the solidarity of a single state. Because of this, far from promoting tax competition, the powers-that-be are driving towards tax harmonisation. The prevalent idea behind tax harmonisation is that different tax regimes within the single market create 'unfair competition.' A country with low (particularly corporate) taxes (such as Britain or Ireland) could be accused of beggar thy neighbour policies, just as those countries that used currency devaluations to get out of recession were in the past. Right from the start of EMU, the bias towards fiscal rigidity rather than flexibility was established through the Growth and Stability Pact that placed strict constraints on any euroland politician who might be tempted to balance the lack of flexibility on monetary policy by using fiscal policy counter-cyclically.

The lack of a single state is also preventing the eurozone from building a federal budget large enough to provide the fiscal transfers necessary to bail out ailing regions in the monetary union. Compared with the US federal equivalent of some 19 per cent to 25 per cent, the EU budget is only 1.27 per cent of GDP. Sir Donald McDougall, Chairman of the influential European Commission report of 1977, argues that at least between 5 and 7 per cent of EU GDP would be needed to make the single currency zone work (and probably more given the equivalent figures in other unitary state monetary unions).

The EU, however, has not got any kind of political consensus behind building a larger budget. This sense of political solidarity is present in the US because the US is a single political entity. The citizens of one state are therefore happy for a portion of their tax payments to be used, if necessary, to bail out the citizens of another state that have hit hard times. It is not yet present in Europe because Europe is still made up of independent-minded nation states. Europe is not, in other words, a country.

In the long run, however, there is no doubt that a significant number of Europe's political and economic leaders have in mind a US destination and, whatever the intentions or wishes of others, the logic of the single currency project will take them to the same end-point in any case. Even if a single fiscal policy at federal level were not needed to make monetary union work – which I believe it is – it would still be desirable as a key building block of political union, which is what many passionate Europeans want. After all, a European constitution, a European judicial space, a directly-elected European president and a European army are all actively on the agenda, as is a desire to replace national European representation on international bodies such as the UN security council and the Group of Seven with EU representation.

Yet, because of popular opinion – which baulks at the idea of a single state in Europe – this aim is being pursued covertly. In Britain, the government has consistently sought to play down any fiscal implications of joining monetary union because, as even Ken Clarke has argued, 'tax and spending decisions are a cornerstone of our parliamentary democracy.'

Europhiles perpetually challenge the analysis that the Euro necessarily leads to something close to a single state. They argue that, even if all member states were in the Euro, the EU would continue to be a unique hybrid, based on intergovernmentalism but with a significant supranational element to coordinate policies. There will be no single taxation policy, they argue. They reject the clear message from the history of monetary unions that, unless backed by political union, they lose their raison d'être, destabilise and break up.

The evidence, however, is wholly in the other direction and, if the final destination of the eurozone is a single monetary and fiscal policy, the overarching question of self-government comes into play. If monetary and fiscal policies are both 'pooled' to a European level, how much of self-government is left?

Ireland has already found that, inside monetary union, its ability to make independent tax and spending decisions is under threat. Pro-Euro campaigners insist that Ireland faces no penalties but merely a new system of 'peer pressure.' However, it is hard to see a situation in which every member state in the eurozone were able continually to defy the 'collective good' before a more concrete system of rules and sanctions were to be formulated and imposed.

Developments on the fiscal side of the EMU equation raise legitimate questions of direct relevance to the current Labour government. At the core of the project now is a steady increase in the amount of money available to key public services. This programme does not necessarily mean that Britain would fall foul of Maastricht limits on budget deficits (if Brown keeps to his golden rule and finances investment only out of receipts, not extra borrowing).

However, at the same Ecofin meeting at which Ireland was reprimanded, Gordon Brown was told that his plans might, within EMU, fall foul of EU rules. For most British voters, this was enormously significant. Labour was re-elected on two main platforms: its handling of the economy and its promise to plough more money into public services. Inside the Euro, neither of these might apply. The British Chancellor would no longer be free to make the major decisions of economic policy and he would not be free to carry out his own spending promises.

I believe that the loss of control over all the major levers of economic power – and the fact that the Euro acts as a powerful catalyst towards political integration – dwarfs any of the claimed benefits of joining monetary union, the removal of exchange rate uncertainty being the prime one (and probably the only one that has some validity). Those countries that do a great deal of trade with other partners in the eurozone will clearly feel the benefit. For Britain, which does less than half of its total trade with the EU, this is not clear-cut. Even Adair Turner, former chief of the Confederation of British Industry and a Euro enthusiast, argues that the advantage of removing currency fluctuations and the disadvantage of living with a single interest rate are finely balanced.

So, the economics of EMU are risky and the politics are heavily integrationist. The next question that needs to be tackled is whether the vision of European unity that has always been the driving force of the EU is inspiring enough to override such misgivings. Many Europeans believe in the eventual aim of a federal state and are prepared – as many visionaries have done in the past – to push it forward despite popular misgivings. Even the sceptical British, as future generations travel and work more in Europe, may enthusiastically back a single state some time in the future. But for now, there is no unanimity about the desire of a federal state, even among those politicians and bureaucrats who have invested so much of their personal capital in the European idea.

There is, in fact, a huge tussle going on in Europe between the intergovernmental and the supranational. At the moment, the nation states – and I would support this – appear to be in the ascendant but this spectacle has not been edifying. The Nice summit in autumn 2000 saw neither the final victory of the European Commission so feared by radical anti-federalists; neither did it see constructive cooperation among the EU's nation states. The summit was an elongated, bitter and ultimately futile war of attrition between different member states and the peoples of Europe reacted with horror.

It is not an exaggeration to say that the EU – as a concept and in reality – has run into very choppy waters indeed. One of the most potent critiques of the current direction of the Union – taking the Euro out of the equation for a moment – is that its structures are simply not

JANET BUSH

democratic and a European polity without democracy will never command popular consent. Some of the most passionate europhiles acknowledge that the EU is facing a 'crisis of legitimacy' with a widening gap between the aspirations of its rulers and the ruled. The 'project' is being built with very little popular consent and well in advance of the instincts and wishes of ordinary Europeans. None of the existing members of the eurozone were given a referendum on joining the Euro and the only country that has so far had a referendum – Denmark – has voted no. Turn out at elections to the European Parliament has steadily fallen and recent opinion polls have found that the EU is getting less popular among the peoples across Europe. There is a real danger that the direct democratic link between the people and those that they vote into power is being destroyed.

In Britain, this is an issue that unites democrats from all political persuasions. Nobody is arguing that Westminster commands the love or respect of many voters – there is an increasing distrust with politicians and increasing evidence that political activism is raging outside the party political structure as people 'do it for themselves.' However, it remains the case that Westminster is more accountable and closer to the electorate than the supranational institutions based in Brussels and Strasbourg.

It is bizarre, in a British context, that power has partially been devolved to Scotland, Wales and to Northern Ireland but that the Government has no political or constitutional concerns about devolving the power of the British government to a pooled sovereignty in Europe. The Labour Party is promising regional assemblies to bring democracy closer to people. Yet at the same time it is advocating that true power should move further away.

Beyond concerns about the democratic deficit, there is a queasy feeling among passionate Europeans about the ethos that drives the current leaders in Europe. Are they committed to a diverse, open-minded, internationalist Europe? Or are they driving towards homogeneity and turning inwards as they pursue their dream of building a new superpower, as Tony Blair described it in a speech in Warsaw last autumn?

A suggested answer to these questions comes from the experience so far of those countries from central and eastern Europe who want to 'return to Europe' by acceding to the EU. The enlargement of the Union to the east is, in essence, about reuniting Europe, an aim that boasts an idealism about our collective European future that has far more resonance than whether a grocer in the north of England is required to sell his vegetables in metric, rather than imperial, measures. Yet the process has been un-edifying and is by no means sure to succeed: the European Commission officials working on enlargement are called 'the grave diggers' by their colleagues.

The accession negotiations have been inflexible and one-sided. The only question has been what the EU is prepared to offer the post-Soviet bloc. There has been no excitement about what these vibrant new democracies, with their new embrace of entrepreneurial dynamism, can bring to us. The entry fee has been set prohibitively high. Every accession country has to fulfil an onerous set of obligations from the 40,000 item acquis communautaire to a raft of economic reforms and eventually compliance with the Maastricht Treaty, an agreement to sign up to all European Union treaties, past and present, with no hope of permanent opt-outs. This means that the accession countries have to sign up to the aim of 'ever closer union' and also to joining EMU. What they get in return is shabby – free movement of capital to their countries but no free movement of labour in the other direction. And nobody is prepared to reform the Common Agricultural Policy if it means spreading subsidies more fairly. On such unfair terms, enlargement may happen, but it will be socially and politically unsustainable.

Despite deep – even critical concerns – there is everything to play for in the EU. Its political structures can, with imagination, be democratised. In time, Europe's peoples can be re-enthused. Perhaps enlargement will, after all, be achieved. Developments in the autumn of 2000 left Europe at a crossroads that affords us an opportunity to pause and take stock of the European project and reconnect the people with our political masters.

The No vote in the Danish referendum on the Euro has opened up a real possibility that not even all the current members of the EU will join the Euro. This creates at least a two-tier but probably a multi-tier Europe. On top of this, the Nice summit achieved two important goals. Firstly, it agreed the necessary institutional change to pave the way for the enlargement of the Union to 30 plus members. It also agreed provisions that will allow groups of countries to 'go off and do their own thing' under enhanced cooperation. The countries that have adopted the Euro are likely to want to move towards far greater economic and political integration for the reasons I have explained. But those countries that do not want to integrate so deeply no longer have to move in lock step with all other members of the EU.

A new Europe – diverse, flexible, cooperating but not metamorphosing into a single state – may now be on offer. It remains the case, however, that 'ever closer union' remains in the EU Treaties and that there is still a presumption that all member states will head for the same end-point, albeit at different speeds. Part of this presumption is that everyone should join EMU. But if this were to happen, Europe would unarguably shift once again away from a multi-tier to a single-tier – or federal – system.

It may seem outlandish to those in Britain who see nothing but post-imperialist, post-war failure that Britain could therefore play a pivotal role in securing a flexible, popular, diverse and dynamic EU. If Britain were to remain outside the Euro, so too might Denmark and Sweden. It is possible that, if EU membership did not automatically involve joining EMU, countries such as Norway and Switzerland might be more inclined to join the EU. And it would be far easier – and less mutually destabilising – to bring in those central and eastern countries that want to join the Union and so 'return to Europe.' Perversely, by being the 'awkward partner,' Britain could make Europe a better, rather than a worse, place.

We, in New Europe, believe that no decision on the Euro should be taken until at least 2004 when another inter-governmental conference is scheduled to discuss a constitution for Europe. I have little confidence that a final settlement of the balance between the EU's nation states and the pan-European institutions will be reached at that point but at least we may have more of a notion of how the EU will look in 10 to 20 years' time. The Euro referendum should wait until 2005 so that the British people can make an informed judgement on where EMU will lead us – politically.

The only argument against 'wait and see' would be if Britain were suffering – economically or politically – by staying out of EMU for now. There is no evidence that it is.

Tell anybody the economic facts about Britain and, so great is the loss of post-war confidence, they tend not to believe you. Britain is the fourth largest economy in the world. Britain has one of the lowest inflation rates in Europe and much lower unemployment than the euroland average. Britain is far better placed to meet its future pensions obligations than most European countries. Britain has a trade surplus with the EU. Britain attracts more foreign direct investment than Germany and France put together and has continued to do so despite (or perhaps because) Britain is outside the Euro. Britain is by far the biggest investor overseas of any country in the world, including America, accounting for one quarter of all world outward investment. High tech engineering has grown by 50 per cent in three years. Britain's long-term interest rates are now as low as the Euroland average. Prosperity is unevenly distributed but overall Britain is doing well and we should have the confidence to make a positive – rather than a defensive choice based on out-of-date perceptions of economic decline – about the Euro.

Nor is Britain suffering politically. The pro-Euro lobby often argues that only by joining the Euro will Britain be able to maximise its influence in Europe. But, on the vast amount of EU business that is unconnected with the Euro, we shall be just as influential as before. In the world at large, much British influence in the world has little or no connection with the Union. Unlike all other member states except France, Britain's assets, interests and influence are spread worldwide. We are, of course, no longer a global power but we have global interests and responsibilities, the latter deriving from our permanent seat on the UN Security Council and our membership of the G8. Neither of these would be threatened by staying out of the Euro. In fact, inside a centralising eurozone, the EU would seek to replace national representation on both the Security Council and the G8 with an EU representative. In this case, Britain's voice and influence would clearly be diminished.

'Not as things now stand' may not be much of a rallying call but it is a rational response to the pressure being exerted to join a project which looks economically risky, that leads us in a political direction that we may not want to go and inflicts no damage on us if we say no.

Chapter 13

Why Britain should join the Euro

by Christopher Huhne MEP

Editor's Comments

It says much for the reputation of the Fourth Estate that two of our contributors who are former professional journalists, now more politically involved, should be among the fairest in terms of examining the arguments with which they disagree. Although they reach opposite conclusions, Janet Bush and **Chris Huhne** *do not simply assert their case, but argue it with respect for the other side – and for you, dear reader and future arbiter. Chris Huhne believes that joining the Euro would bring economic benefits to Britain, but disagrees with Janet Bush in seeing real cause for concern at the loss of political influence outside the single currency, to the extent that freedom would be a myth. He is sceptical about the feared appetite for a super-state in Europe.*

Why Britain should join the Euro

by Christopher Huhne MEP

The British, by temperament, prefer small and gradual changes. Over time these changes may build up, but there should be nothing too dramatic or revolutionary if we can help it. EMU was therefore everything that British policymakers usually dislike. It was a large, dramatic, discontinuous and radical change. Indeed, it has been the largest change in international monetary arrangements since the Bretton Woods system after the second world war. It is arguably the largest single change in the framework of economic policy that has ever been tried in Europe, including Bretton Woods and the gold standard.

What is, however, incontrovertible is that monetary union has happened, and it has happened on a much larger scale than most British policymakers, let alone the eurosceptics, ever believed possible. With 11 founding members now joined in 2001 by Greece, the Euro is now used by 301 million people. It is a currency area of similar size to the United States, with a similar weight on the world economic stage. Moreover, thirteen candidate countries are queuing to join the EU. All will eventually adopt the Euro as their currency, and several of them want to do so as soon as possible.

This new reality fundamentally alters the status quo. Until January 1st 1999, the pound was just another European currency among many. But now it is a comparatively small currency set against a vast one, the movements of which completely dominate the inflationary impact of import prices and the competitiveness of British exporters. The potential for great volatility in sterling has increased, particularly since the relationship between the Euro and the dollar is itself likely to be more volatile as their respective monetary authorities care little about their exchange rates (since they affect only a small part of their now continent-wide economies). Given that international capital flows are also increasing inexorably – a trend that is likely to continue with the growth of private pensions – the potential for the pound to be squeezed between the great tectonic plates of Europe and America has never been greater. It will not be comfortable. The familiar post-war association of 'sterling' and 'crisis' is not over yet.

In this context Britain cannot merely opt out and pretend that nothing is happening. If we are to stay out of the Euro we must expect an even bumpier ride than we have had over the last 25 years of a largely floating exchange rate for sterling. We will need to reinforce the credibility of our monetary institutions, which will otherwise bear unfavourable comparison with those of the United States and Euro-area.[1] We will also have to ensure that fiscal policy remains on track, as the cost of market punishment will be greater outside the Euro than inside it. Not only can bond yields rise if the markets disapprove of a government's policy, but the exchange rate can fall. Moreover, the exchange rate may well come under strain because of developments in either the United States or Euro-area and require offsetting fiscal and interest-rate changes to compensate. After all, the Deutschmark/pound exchange rate dropped to just DEM2.2 in 1995 and went into over-drive in 2000 hitting DM3.45, helping to cause more than a third of a million unnecessary job losses among manufacturers.

In this world, the balance of costs and benefits points to British entry into the Euro-area. The costs are often overstated. The divergences that have in the past occurred among the European economies – the problem that a one-size-fits-all monetary policy is meant to aggravate – have already been experienced in other monetary unions, notably the United States but also existing European countries. Indeed, Britain's economic performance is more closely related to the continent's than, say, East Anglia's and Northern Ireland's are to Britain's. If Britain cannot share a currency with Europe, then the same logic should suggest that several parts of Britain should have their own pound.[2] In truth, eurosceptic assertions about the impossibility of sharing an interest rate are disproved daily. European inflation rates are within the range traditionally seen in the United States, and the Euro has had a dramatically beneficial effect on growth and jobs. The Euro-area has been growing more quickly than Britain for nearly three years, registered its highest growth rate for ten years in 2000, and has created a net 5.36 million new jobs since the beginning of the system. Indeed, job creation has been running at double the British or American growth rate.

In truth, an independent monetary policy (both interest rates and exchange rate) is a diminishing asset in an increasingly interdependent world. Moreover, it is wrong to assume that the freedoms an independent policy affords are unalloyed benefits. Sterling is not, as the eurosceptics would have us believe, an essential part of a country's economic tool-kit. Indeed, many of the greatest shocks administered to the British economy over the post-war period have been home-grown instances of ill-judged policy, including far greater and more sudden shocks to our trading sectors (such as manufacturing in 1979–81) created by sterling than are imaginable in EMU. The lack of an independent exchange rate and interest rate will put pressure on the remaining means of adjustment – the labour market – but this is already more flexible than it was, and Britain is certainly as well able to adjust as other large EMU participants. Contrary to conventional wisdom, Britain's economy is not disproportionately affected by short-term interest rates, despite the importance of variable-rate mortgages. This is because when interest rates rise, savers benefit too, offsetting the losses to borrowers.

On the benefits side, British consumers will have more choice and greater ease in comparing prices. This will end the phenomenon of rip-off Britain that allows Coca-Cola to charge double here what it charges in Spain[3], or Ford to charge 65 per cent more for a Focus than in Denmark.[4] For far too long, multi-national companies have known Britain as 'Treasure Island' because of our willingness to pay through the nose.[5] Any company that tries to make those high price differences stick if we join the Euro-area is going to find that enterprising traders will buy in bulk in other parts of the Euro-area, and import back into Britain. At present, the risk that sterling may move against them is a serious disincentive to invest heavily in the trade. But the Euro will create a US-style single market for the first time. In short, the Euro is the way of ensuring that competitive pressures will increase, driving prices in Britain down to the Euro-area average.

For businesses, British adoption of the Euro will increase efficiency. True, businesses will have to fight harder to make a profit as a result of increased competition. But businesses will be able to redesign their production and logistics systems to take advantage of the lowest costs in the Euro-area, regardless of exchange rate considerations. This is perhaps the most fundamental step forward, albeit often underestimated by our macro-economically obsessed policymakers. The Euro is already making a reality of the single European market and providing businesses with opportunities for economies of scale of which they can at present only dream. It is not an accident that there tend to be fewer, larger competing companies in the US market compared with Europe's fragmented industrial structure. But the single market, completed by the Euro, is increasing prospective returns on investment, and thereby growth and jobs. There will also be an elimination of the transactions costs in moving from the pound to the Euro. Britain can and should participate in these gains.

Indeed, there may be a long-term cost if we do not. There is a parallel between Britain's failure to participate in the Euro today and our failure to join the European Union in 1958. The single currency is analogous to the market-opening tariff reductions of the early years of the EU, which gave French and German industry such enormous benefits by ensuring that they faced increased competition. By contrast, British businesses did not have to adjust to a more competitive world until the seventies, and paid a high price for foregoing those years of incremental improvement. Delayed change eventually means more radical and disruptive change. As Sir Geoffrey Owen has written, in his magisterial overview of Britain's relative economic decline in the post-war period, 'the biggest single mistake was to opt out of European integration in the 1950s.'[6] We should not repeat it today.

The second mechanism by which EMU delivers important benefits is through the reduction of risks, particularly exchange-rate uncertainty. This may be expected to boost trade flows, but, even more crucially, it is already boosting investment across borders within EMU and raising the long-run growth rate of the European Union. Portugal, for example, is now importing capital worth more than 10 per cent of GDP each year without ill effects, even though such a flow under floating exchange rates created a monstrous currency crisis for the escudo, followed by a sharp recession. By creating a monetary area that is a continent-wide economy, EMU has insulated its member economies from external shocks caused either by problems in other economies or by financial flows and mis-aligned exchange rates. Britain's membership would lift the constraint which British policymakers have often felt: the need to ensure that the balance of payments (of exports and imports) does not go too far into deficit. Within EMU the balance of payments can no longer have a traumatic effect on the exchange rate of an individual member state, or on its inflation rate.

EMU also reduces the risks of inflation, and hence cuts interest-rate costs in the long run. The credibility of Europe's monetary institutions is already greater, in the only measurable sense, than that of its American counterparts. Governments whose countries are participating in Euro-area are already able to borrow on better terms over a ten-year period than the American government, owing to the markets' belief that inflation is less likely to erode the value of the debt. True, Britain has already reaped much of this benefit thanks to the independence of the Bank of England. However, there is evidence that real interest rates – interest rates after allowing for inflation – have tended to be higher in Britain than elsewhere regardless of the point of the business cycle. This may reflect a perception of increased risk in the UK, whether due to prospective inflation or a fall in sterling. If Britain joined monetary union, Britain's real interest rates would converge on Euro-area ones, cutting real interest payments. Such a reduction in interest costs could be £38 a month for the average mortgage payer over the business cycle.

Most importantly for our longer-term prospects, businesses should find capital more easily and cheaply just as our Euro-area competitors are doing now. Banks will compete fiercely for new business, and the new capital markets of the Euro area are encouraging the growth of risk capital, particularly in the bond market. These interest rates and financial-market effects will help to reduce the cost of capital in Britain, and therefore boost investment. Lastly, the advent of a new world currency will offer all Europeans the advantage of seignorage: the ability to buy other people's exports and offer them printed banknotes in exchange. The Euro is likely to become a major world currency, used as a store of value, a means of exchange and a unit of account much beyond euroarea.

These general advantages are reinforced by two particular features of Britain's situation, which mean that we may disproportionately benefit from the single currency. The first is our ability to attract foreign direct investment (FDI). If we join this will be underpinned. Indeed, we may benefit from the new wave of investment likely in the early years of EMU. This is of crucial importance to some of Britain's poorest regions – the North and South Wales – that have benefited from Japanese and American inwards investment. Outside EMU, Britain suffers a key disadvantage in attempting to win investment. We cannot promise, unlike EMU members, that the flow of income from an investment producing for the whole European market will not be suddenly revalued or devalued by currency shifts. And most manufacturing investments in Britain aim not just at the British market, but the European one.

The second particular feature of the UK is the position of the City of London as Europe's incipient financial centre. Within EMU London can be more than just a centre of international finance. It can be the centre of the new, integrated Euro capital markets. Thanks to EMU, Europe's financial markets are coming to resemble those of the United States, where just the New York stock exchanges list 3,000 more companies than London, Paris and Frankfurt combined, and where there is four times the amount of share trading as in the three big European exchanges.[7] The City has already been losing market share as the continental centres attract new business, and companies choose to have their shares quoted in Euro-bourses. Outside EMU, the City's role is likely to come under increasing challenge from Paris and Frankfurt.

These unique British factors, the importance of FDI and of the City, are part of the answer to the questions: Why not wait and see how things turn out? Delay always sounds reasonable. EMU has gone ahead with a large membership. The great experiment has begun. But if we wait any longer we also increase the risk of losses because foreign investors go elsewhere, and because other centres pick up business from the City. Nor are we likely to settle the issue by waiting. The sorts of things that might go wrong with EMU are unlikely to happen quickly. They might never happen. They might happen only after 20 years. No one is really suggesting that we can wait that long. Even the 'doctrine of unripe time,' that famous bureaucratic delaying tactic when arguments of principle fail or prove inexpedient, would not sustain British non-membership for such a period.

The government is rightly worried about the loss of political influence within Europe entailed by Britain's non-membership in such an important European project. Our credibility as a whole-hearted member of the club is inevitably in doubt, and this weakens our hand in many negotiations that concern our future prosperity. Why make some special effort of concession to Britain when it may not even be a full member in ten years time? Yet EU legislation that crucially determines the market opportunities available to leading UK companies – for example, the effort to establish a single market in financial services – will be settled by 2005. And in 2004, there will be another intergovernmental conference designed to put final shape on the institutions of the EU. Our lateness in joining the Euro has already cost London the seat of the European Central Bank. By joining the EU late in 1973, we had to accept many institutional arrangements that might have been far more comfortable if we had been able to negotiate changes when they came about, notably the Common Agricultural Policy and the Common Fisheries Policy. What costs will there still be to come if we continue to delay on the Euro?

If you believe, as most British people seem to believe according to the opinion polls, that British membership of the Euro is merely a matter of time, then it is supremely irrational to delay. We will, when we join, have to pay all the upfront costs (such as conversion costs for slot machines) in any case. But with each month that passes we are delaying the benefits. If an investment is worth undertaking, it is worth undertaking as soon as possible so as to bring the benefits on stream. British membership of EMU is precisely such a case. We will make the investment before long, so it makes no sense to delay the benefits.

The eurosceptics increasingly recognise the power of this logic as they flail to find an alternative vision for Britain and its economy in the 21st century. This is one reason Conrad Black, the Canadian proprietor of the Telegraph newspapers, recently wrote an interesting article in his own journal, entitled 'Britain's final choice: Europe or America?,' which rather let the cat out of the bag.[8] Mr Black argued that Britain should leave the European Union and become a member of the North American Free Trade Agreement (NAFTA). 'If the United States received a signal from a British government that it wished to avail itself of a North American option, they would respond immediately,' he wrote. 'If America were jubilant, Canada would be ecstatic.' So there is a secret agenda, but is not on the part of the pro-Europeans; it is the secret agenda of the anti-Europeans, which is to leave the European Union.

This is, of course, a rich newspaper proprietor's whimsy since the Americans have pushed hardest for British membership of the European Union, and take British views seriously in exact proportion to our influence in Europe.[9] For free traders, there is a good argument for trying to negotiate an Atlantic Free Trade Area (AFTA) including both the EU and NAFTA.[10] But the argument that we should abandon the EU to join NAFTA is extraordinary. The cost of shipping a 40 foot cube container from Canterbury to the nearest port on the European mainland – Calais – is £450 whereas the cost of the same shipment to Boston – the nearest port in the US – is £1,540. Transport costs between Britain and NAFTA are three times as high as transport costs between Britain and the EU, and these costs dwarf tariffs. Inevitably, we will have a much closer trading relationship with our European partners than with the North Americans. Since we export nearly three times as much to the EU as to NAFTA, we would end up paying far more tariffs on EU exports than we would save on NAFTA exports particularly since two thirds of our trade with NAFTA is tariff free in any case. The amount of competition for the consumers' pound would be reduced, and we would give a whole new meaning to 'rip off Britain.'

The idea that leaving the European Union would allow us to 'regain control' over our own concerns is also absurd. It completely fails to understand the globalised world in which we live. Norway is outside the EU, but its businesses need to sell in the EU, which is their largest market. As a result, Norway has introduced 3,000 items of EU legislation covering industrial standards, consumer safety requirements and environmental measures needed to ensure that its products comply with EU rules, and can have unfettered access to the single market. Yet the Norwegians have no influence over any of these rules in either the Council of Ministers or the European Parliament, because Norwegians are not represented. If that is what our europhobes mean by national sovereignty, they should think again. We should never exchange the illusion of sovereignty outside the EU for the reality of power within it.

Leaving aside the question of oceanography, the problem for most British people with Conrad Black's vision is that we have no more desire to become an appendage of the United States than to be subsumed into a European superstate. Yet recently a legal case brought by the US-based Ethyl Corporation under the NAFTA rules caused the Canadian Parliament to repeal a law designed to protect its environment. There are six other similar cases. In NAFTA, legal processes supersede political ones. By contrast, the European Union, which celebrates its cultural, social and ethnic diversity, suits British interests well. Most people realise that the threat to Britain's cultural identity does not come from Brussels, but from our seductive cousins across the Atlantic with their all-conquering Hollywood dream factory. British social values are more European than American, as is reflected in our relatively strong commitment to a welfare state and to relatively high provision of public services. Most British people know that there is no conflict between being British, English and a Yorkshire person. To be European is just another layer of our identity.

Since the eurosceptics have no alternative vision to offer as a way of imposing public choices on the increasingly globalised world in which we live, they resort instead to creating scare stories, asserting that monetary union will lead to a 'federal superstate.' In fact, there are many examples of monetary unions without political unions: Luxembourg with Belgium since 1921 is only one of some 95 monetary unions around the world, most without any political superstructure. From 1921 to 1979, the Irish were also in monetary union with Britain, although no-one would argue that this either undermined the Irish national identity or led to political union. Indeed, President Eamonn de Valera redrafted the Irish constitution to stress the differences with the United Kingdom but the monetary link continued. And he exercised ultimate sovereignty by remaining neutral when Britain was at war, but the monetary union continued. The Maastricht framework for monetary union is similarly minimalist.

Indeed, the debate in the run-up to the negotiation on the new Treaty of Nice shows clearly how little appetite there is for any such super-state. First, the existing European institutions remain a small part of the totality of Europe's public sectors, with a budget accounting for 1.11 per cent of GDP in 2000 compared with 46 per cent of GDP spent by all levels of government. The Commission employs 23,000 people, fewer than half the number of Birmingham City Council with 56,000 staff. Secondly, the outstanding total of legislation at the European level has remained surprisingly static over the last ten years. True, there was an increase in EU law in the late eighties to establish the single market (with common safety measures and standards). But the twin legislative chambers, the EU Council of Ministers and the European Parliament, have repealed as much as they have put on the statute book since that time. Thirdly, the member states that have been the greatest motors of integration – France and Germany – are hesitant in pressing for more. It is a paradox, given the German rhetoric in favour of political union, that Germany blocked an extension of majority voting in the Amsterdam inter-governmental conference, and that France had more objections to new areas of majority voting than any other member state in the Nice intergovernmental conference. To even the most hardened eurosceptic, the Nice summit and treaty were surely proof that the nation states remain in Europe's driving seat. Germany now wants a final treaty in 2004 to draw the limits to the European level of government, abandoning the commitment to 'ever closer union.'

The real point is not whether Britain will lose sovereignty by giving up the pound, but whether we will gain some control over our economic environment that we would not otherwise have by pooling it. We cannot long stand aside from the central project of the European Union, already adopted by 13 other member states and soon to be adopted as a matter of course by the 13 candidate members in central and Eastern Europe. The Euro is a big change, but it has come to seem a much smaller one in the context of present hyperactive international markets. Do we want to live in a world where exchange rates can be so buffeted by speculation that they can move by nearly 10 per cent in one trading session, and where the reasonable expectations of our exporters can be overturned in a week?

Lord Keynes warned that the financial system should never allow the bubbles and froth of speculation to undermine the steady efforts of commerce and industry. He was right. We need to use our sovereignty to provide a stable environment for our businesses, in the same way that we have rightly used our sovereignty to provide a secure defence within NATO. What sort of freedom is it to hike interest rates so high to defend your exchange rate that you drive the economy into recession? What sort of freedom is it to float your exchange rate and price hundreds of thousands out of work? What sort of freedom is it to run bad policies and a high inflation rate? The freedoms on offer if we stay outside the Euro turn out, on close inspection, not to be freedoms at all. The benefits, on the other hand, are tangible for consumers, businesses, borrowers, investors and jobs. In the real world, the Euro can help deliver a more assured prosperity than can only be threatened outside.

Notes

[1] For a clear assessment of the options, including what needs to happen if we stay out of the Euro, see the report of an independent panel chaired by Rupert Pennant-Rea, CEPR (1997)

[2] See Huhne, Christopher *Both sides of the coin: the case for the Euro and European monetary union*, 2nd edition, June 2001, Profile books. (The case against written by James Forder).

[3] Bureau European des Unions de Consommateurs, comparison in July 1998.

[4] EU Commission competition directorate general, comparison of 2000 car prices.

[5] According to the *Sunday Times* of 15 April 2001, branded goods are a particular problem. Taking a comparison of Nike women's trainers, Chanel no 5 perfume, Ralph Lauren polo shirt, Sony Playstation 2 game and Levi's 501 jeans, Britain was the most expensive country in every case. Prices were 16 per cent lower in Germany, 13 per cent lower in France and 37 per cent lower in Spain.

[6] Owen, Geoffrey, *From Empire to Europe: the decline and revival of British industry since the second world war*, London, Harper-Collins, 1999

[7] see Mathias Levin 'The Euro and the City,' *The City in Europe* (forthcoming in 2001).

[8] Extracts from 'Britain's final choice: Europe or America?,' a speech by Conrad Black at the annual meeting of the Centre for Policy Studies, *Daily Telegraph*, July 10th, 1998

[9] As the former US ambassador to Britain, Mr Raymond Seitz, has said: 'If Britain's voice is less influential in Paris or Bonn, it is likely to be less influential in Washington.'

[10] AFTA would make sense particularly since the residual tariffs are no longer very high following successive trade liberalisation rounds. The EU common external tariff averages 4.9 per cent while the US tariff averages 3.2 per cent.

Chapter 14

Valid Consent, not mere persuasion: A Referendum on European Government

by Bill Cash MP

Editor's Commentary

*One thing all contributors agree on in some measure (and most of them completely) is that the referendum will, however the question is phrased, be about more than just whether we should join the Euro: it will be about Britain's future relationship with the European Union. No-one holds this view more fundamentally than **Bill Cash**, another consistent opponent of British membership: indeed he would prefer the referendum specifically to pose the wider question of European Government. He fears the real issue is the threat to British democracy posed by the movement towards ever-closer European integration of which the single currency is just a part, and he calls for the Treaties to be renegotiated.*

Valid consent, not mere persuasion: A Referendum on European Government

by Bill Cash MP[1]

I believe that the single most important duty a politician owes his country is to fight for democracy. If democracy is under threat, the politician should fight to defend it; if democracy has been taken away, the politician should fight to recover it. I have argued for years now in countless articles, pamphlets, books and speeches that the gradual movement towards ever-closer European integration represents the greatest threat to our democracy since that the Second World War. That is why I oppose the construction of the European state, why I opposed the Treaties of Maastricht and Amsterdam and why I am fighting to prevent the ratification of the Nice Treaty.

The European debate is thus fundamentally about answering the following political question: who should govern Britain? Should it be the British people through their elected representatives (from Parish councillors to Members of the Westminster Parliament)? Or should it be the unelected, unaccountable, even unknown bureaucrats and 'judges' of the European Commission, the European Court of Justice and the other EU institutions? This is the question to which the British people will have to answer one way or the other sometime in the next few years. I will argue in this paper that to hold a referendum on the Euro alone would be to deceive the British people: the referendum will only be valid if it addresses the much wider question of European government.

Why the EU will always be undemocratic

It is well know that the term 'democracy' is derived from the Greek *demos* (the people) and *kratos* (power). Europe has plenty of *kratos* but no single *demos* – its diversity of language, culture, political history and outlook must surely be the European continent's most striking and endearing characteristic. Although there is a concerted movement to use propaganda and cultural policy to create a new European people[2] – an 'imagined community' if ever there were one[3] – such a monumental act of social engineering would at the very least take decades before it bore any fruits. As such, democracy is impossible by definition in Europe: the European institutions will never be democratic, however much one tinkers with the European Parliament to imbue it with spurious legitimacy. The absence of a single 'European' culture as compared to the range of its different cultures means that there is no single European media to relay to the people what is happening politically and to help hold politicians to account.

More practically, all sides on the European issue agree that there is no forum for holding the European Commission to account. Furthermore, the emasculation of the Westminster Parliament combined with the excesses of the whip system in the UK mean that increasingly the executive is all powerful, and there is no way to hold the Council of Ministers to account either.

It is the principle of democracy which is so important. Very few people understand in the abstract what it means for a country to be 'sovereign' but everyone understands what 'democracy' means: the right for ordinary people to kick out their rulers at regular intervals when, for whatever reason, they get tired of them. We need to have a referendum on democracy – on who governs Britain.

The Euro is only part of the problem

It is important to identify the role of Economic and Monetary Union in this context. The new European government is taking on a number of concrete manifestations: we have a nascent European army, a nascent European Police Force, a European currency, a European system of taxation, and many other Euro-policies besides. In other words, the Euro is just one of the many branches of a new European government – a very important branch, certainly, but by no means the only one. Crucially, although this would certainly have very important economic consequences, whether or not we should adopt the Euro remains a fundamentally political question – to abolish the pound would be to vest more power with the EU and to give up more of our self-government.[4]

This is why I believe that it would be a disaster for eurorealists in this country to fall into the trap of 'totem pole politics' and become fixated with defeating the Euro while neglecting everything else. I would go as far as to argue that some on my side of the debate have made the Euro into another Maginot line: we shall pour all our resources into defending this one front, they say, and we shall defeat the forces of federalism for ever. If we do this we risk winning the Euro-battle but losing the Euro-war because rejecting the Euro is at best a temporary palliative which would do nothing to reverse the ever-growing encroachment of the Treaties.

EMU is not only about the Euro

Most people believe that EMU and the Euro are synonymous. At the root of the problem is confusion about the 'E' in EMU: it stands for Economic, not European (although one can certainly talk of European Economic and Monetary Union.) Far from being a trivial point of semantics, this goes to the heart of the entire European debate and explains why the referendum should be on the broader question of who should govern us. Our so-called Maastricht 'opt-out' only applies to Stage III of EMU. We have already 'opted-into' Stages I and II which include a number of restrictive macroeconomic fiscal rules and from which we will need to extract ourselves.

One essential issue emerges from the row over Brussels's interference with the fiscal policies of the United Kingdom and Ireland. If voters want their governments to retain ultimate control over such matters as classroom sizes, waiting lists, police cuts and public service pensions, the Maastricht Treaty and the Stability and Growth Pact must be renegotiated. Our current problems stem from Title VII on Economic and Monetary Policy in the Consolidated Treaty Establishing the European Community (TEC). The relevant articles therefore include article 98 to 124, with a number of exceptions for those countries such as the UK which are not currently in Stage III, and no exceptions for countries such as Ireland that are already in Stage III. For example, article 116 states that 'each Member State shall adopt [...] multiannual programmes intended to ensure the lasting convergence necessary for the achievement of economic and monetary union, in particular with regard to price stability and sound public finances.' Furthermore, the Treaties also stipulate conditions governing deficit control under the terms of the Stability and Growth Pact (SGP). It is clearly stated that whereas the obligation to avoid excessive general government deficits 'does not apply to the United Kingdom unless it moves to the third stage; the obligation under Article 109(e) (4) [now Article 116] of the Treaty establishing the European Community to endeavour to avoid excessive deficits shall continue to apply to the United Kingdom.'

A referendum on the whole of EMU would be a referendum on large sections of Maastricht, Amsterdam and Nice. A 'no' vote on EMU as a whole would seriously damage the EU's plans for currency unification, tax harmonisation and total expenditure control and would force an emergency Intergovernmental Conference. A 'no' vote on the Euro alone would do no such thing and would merely maintain the status quo on Stage III while doing nothing to derail the automatic process towards further centralisation of power in other areas inbuilt in the EU treaties and the Brussels machine. Nevertheless, a referendum on the whole of EMU would still be insufficient because large sections of Maastricht, Amsterdam and Nice would remain untouched.

The connection between the European and the domestic agenda

Although Britain's government is increasingly located outside the British Isles, opinion polls regularly come to the conclusion that although the population is overwhelmingly opposed to the Euro, people do not really care that much about 'Europe' in general. They are more concerned with problems such as rampant crime, the lamentable state of the NHS and poor schools. But as we have just seen in the case of EMU, the EU actually controls or influences a far greater proportion of domestic policy than most people realise. Foot and Mouth disease is a case in point. The trick is to make the connection with the fundamental European dimension of all these issues to show that the Treaties are not some irrelevant abstraction – they actually have a massive impact on daily lives. In the case of Foot and Mouth, the media have generally failed to highlight that Nick Brown, de jure our agriculture minister, is de facto little more than a spokesman for the Commission. The truth of the matter is that a whole raft of EU directives regulating food standards, animal health including vaccination, abattoirs and the control of water pollution mean that the British government has only relative control over Foot and Mouth. For example, the main directive on the matter says that 'member states shall ensure that the use of foot and mouth vaccines is prohibited [...] the storage, supply, distribution and sale of foot and mouth vaccines on the territory of the Community are carried out under official control.'[5] The document adds as a caveat that the Commission might take the decision to introduce emergency vaccination for short periods of time in certain cases.[6]

A referendum on European integration

We need a referendum on the whole issue of European integration, a referendum to decide who should control our defence, our taxes, our justice and our currency. There must be a reopening of the mistaken policies of the past, a full and proper and honest explanation of what is at stake, a clear analysis of the issues and the procedures which have to be followed and finally a clear policy of renegotiation. To this end, I believe that we must exorcise the 1972 White Paper which so misled the British people by calling for a new White Paper on the full constitutional and political implications European integration. This would need to explain exactly what powers have already been ceded to the EU, the effectiveness of Parliamentary scrutiny over European law-making, the true relationship between the Council of Ministers and our government and Parliament, the remaining extent of the national veto, the role of the European Court of Justice and the impact of the European army, to mention but a few areas. Following that, a referendum should be held. Although we have all become used to the idea of an exclusively Euro-referendum, the idea is comparatively very recent. To understand why this is so important, it is necessary to take a look at the history of the EU referendum movement in Britain. The 1975 campaign was fought on the whole range of issues including free trade, our relationship with the Commonwealth and high food prices. In the early 1990s, despite the massive petition to Parliament organised and collected by the Maastricht Referendum Campaign (MARC), John Major failed to give us a referendum on Maastricht. Eurorealists MPs on both sides of the House repeatedly tabled amendments and presented Bills calling for a referendum on the Treaty (not just on Economic and Monetary Union). Though the hereditary peers were still at the time members of the House of Lords, John Major's government whipped the upper House into submission. It voted 470 to 176 against Lord Blake's amendment which would have provided a much needed opportunity to consult the people. By June 1996 I had gained the cross-party support of 95 MPs for a Referendum Bill. It went through on a division though of course in the end nothing came of it. Sir James Goldsmith's intervention beginning in 1996 and peaking during the 1997 election campaign was another major attempt to achieve a referendum on who governs Britain. Even when all three party leaders had promised to hold a referendum on Euro membership, Sir James refused to back down. His campaign was not only concerned with the issue of whether or not we should enter Stage III of Economic and Monetary Union and he realised that they were just trying to buy him off. Unfortunately, many commentators and even parts of the eurorealist movement failed to see this and to this day believe they won an important victory. In reality, although they were forced to put on ice their plans to abolish the pound, the europhile establishment were quick to interpret the decision as a green light to integrate as fast as possible. It was a very clever strategic decision for our opponents to take.

The death of the veto

Another threat to our democratic national self-government comes from the massive extension of the veto since the Maastricht Treaty. The 1971 White Paper on accession to the then Common Market solemnly promised that there was no question of the UK giving up the veto – the Paper rightly argued that this would 'imperil the very fabric of the Community.' That promise was not worth the paper it was printed on: 41 vetoes were abolished at Maastricht, 19 at Amsterdam and up to 43 at Nice (the totals vary depending on how they are tallied).[7] If Nice is ratified then around 90 per cent of decisions – almost all about matters that vitally impact our national interests – will be taken by Qualified Majority Voting. It is no secret that the EU wishes to extend that even further. Speaking to the European Parliament on the 1 December 1999, EU Commission President Romano Prodi said that

> '[a]s long as the veto exists, the EU will be like a soldier trying to march with a ball and chain around one leg. The unanimity requirement means either complete paralysis or reducing everything to the lowest common denominator. It is simply a non-starter in today's world.'

British influence on the wane

There were many such examples of further loss of UK control at the Nice IGC in December 2000, as a result of the long-planned changes to the weighting of votes in the Council of Ministers and in the European Parliament.

As I pointed out to Keith Vaz during a European Scrutiny Committee, it is not true that Britain's influence has somehow been increased in the European Parliament and the Council, as the British government has repeatedly claimed. Basic arithmetic is sufficient to demonstrate the absurdity of this claim. In the Council of Ministers, Britain's share of the votes has fallen from 10/87 – equivalent to 11.5 per cent of the votes – to 29/345, equivalent to 8.4 per cent of the votes. In the European Parliament, Britain's share has declined from 87/626 – equivalent to 13.9 per cent of the votes – to 74/732, which comes to a paltry 10.1 per cent. Furthermore, Britain will lose a Commissioner. (Each member state will appoint one Commissioner until there are the number of members reaches 27. After that, some countries will have to take it in turns to have a Commissioner.)

Germany's elite increases its control

A new voting system was introduced at Nice which will especially benefit the German government and upset the balance of power in EU institutions. The new proposed 'Double majority' voting scheme requires two conditions to be met for a decision to be adopted. First, a proposal must garner 258/345 or 74.78 per cent of the votes in the Council of Ministers. Second, the proposal must be backed by countries representing 62 per cent of the EU's population. Thanks to this second clause, Germany and two other large countries – such as France or Italy – will be able to block anything they do not like, whereas Britain will need more than two other countries to vote with her to oppose undesirable decisions. The blocking minority is 88 votes in the Council, which means that Germany would not have been able to block decisions so easily in the absence of the population requirement. The two key initiatives which Nice took – to draw up a European constitution in 2004 and to launch a 'hard core' (also known as 'enhanced cooperation') of states around Germany – mean that, in the words of one German diplomat, 'the direction of European policy for the coming years will be based on two ideas which were originally very German.'[8] On the sensitive issue of double majority, which allows Germany and Germany alone to block EU policies, Mr Schröder said sarcastically 'One could speak of double majority – but one does not have to.' It should be stressed that the German people are among the victims of Nice: their elite has once again failed them by selling out their democracy for personal gain. The German Länder are also increasingly realising that Germany's traditional federal system is rapidly being dismantled by successive EU treaties. Soon, virtually all powers will be held by EU institutions or by the Federal government and the Länder as well as local government will be reduced to making sure the streets are clean. Consequently, many EU observers are rightly calling Chancellor Gerhard Schröder and his political friends the 'victors of Nice.' This success was, says one paper, due to the German elite's tactic of calling for things instead of standing against them. The French, British and Spanish were all determined to defend positions: the Germans, by contrast, stood for change. This allowed the other states to be cornered, because their positions seemed self interested, while the Germans could stand quietly by as the positions of the others were demolished.[9] It is crucial geopolitical issues of this sort that are being brushed under the carpet by the excessive concentration on the issue of the Euro. The British people have the right to be consulted on issues which directly determine what sort of people will be taking decisions for them.

The militarisation of Europe

It is certainly true that he who controls its currency will call much of the tune in Europe. But surely it matters just as much who controls our tanks, guns and above all nuclear arsenal. There is no doubt about it: current moves towards a 'rapid reaction force' as an embryonic integrated EU army are as dangerous as EMU. Europe's military dimension must therefore be as deserving of a referendum as its monetary dimension, but rather than have a whole series of referendums we might as well have an all-inclusive one. The militarisation of the EU has come about following the summits at Feira, St Malo and Cologne and did not actually require any treaty modifications at Nice – Maastricht and Amsterdam provide a perfectly adequate if unsatisfactory treaty base, despite assertions to the contrary. The most interesting and important decisions about defence matters are to be found in the Presidency report on The European Security and Defence Policy and accompanying annexes released after Nice in December 2000. Here are some gems which help to put the argument in perspective:

There will be 'an autonomous capacity to take decisions and action in the security and defence field'

'this development will also lead to a genuine strategic partnership between the EU and Nato in the management of crises with due regard for the two organisations' *decision-making autonomy.'*

The Report has an entire section entitled on *The Establishment of Permanent Political and Military Structures.*

'To enable the European Union fully to assume its responsibilities, the European Council has decided to establish the following permanent political and military bodies, which should be made ready to start their work: the Political and Security Committee; the Military Committee of the European Union; the Military Staff of the European Union'

'The main challenge for member States is to develop military capabilities which can be put at the disposal of the EU for crisis management purposes. The aim is to mobilise Member States' efforts in this sphere.'

The ERRF will engage in 'crisis-management and conflict-prevention capability in support of the objectives of the Common and Foreign Security Policy.'

'Where Nato as a whole is not engaged, to launch and conduct EU-led military operations in response to international crises'

'to carry out the full range of Petersberg tasks [...] humanitarian and rescue tasks, peace-keeping tasks and tasks of combat forces in crisis management, including peacemaking.'

These extracts are particularly interesting. They admit that the two organisations will be entirely separate and that the ERRF will not be some sort of European wing of Nato. It demonstrates that the EU is not merely seeking to take on 'its fair share' of the defence of Europe. Rather, the EU is setting up an entirely new body as a competitor to Nato. The talk of 'strategic partnership' between the two organisations is dangerous wishful thinking: why should America continue to share intelligence secrets and cooperate with the UK if we are using their help to promote and enhance a rival army? The US got burnt in Kosovo when the French allegedly leaked military intelligence to the enemy and senior military commanders understandably do not want this to happen again. The document also goes on to discuss cooperation between the EU and the UN, the OSCE and the Council of Europe, which further proves my point. The Report ads as a somewhat ludicrous caveat – presumably intended for British domestic political consumption – that 'this does not involve the establishment of a European army.' The only sense in which this appears to be true is that no additional resources are being committed to the Rapid Reaction Force other than those already spent on defence by member states. No new soldiers will be recruited, no new warships commissioned and no new planes purchased. The 'Euro-army' will draw on existing personnel and equipment.

We should vote on renegotiation

I have argued in this paper that the EU is inherently undemocratic and that the only solution is to hold a referendum on the wider question of who governs Britain rather than on the Euro. Rather than the two-speed Europe launched by Nice, I believe in a Europe of different spheres. The countries of Europe should be given the choice between belonging to a sphere ruled by European government; or they could join a Associated European Area which would be purely intergovernmental and solely concerned with the promotion of free trade.[10] Following a 'no' result in a referendum on the question of European government, I believe that the United Kingdom would be ideally placed to play a leading role in establishing the Association. An emergency Intergovernmental Conference would have to be called following the referendum and we could invite potentially interested countries to discuss the matter. A handful of treaty amendments would be necessary.[11]

Treaty Amendment I

An amendment allowing the states of the new Associated European Area to be subject retrospectively only to those elements of the acquis communautaire dealing with trade and of cross-border environmental policy managed through intergovernmental channels.

Treaty Amendment II

An amendment allowing the states in the new Associated European Area freely to conclude trade agreements in the absence of action by the European Union as a whole.

Treaty Amendment III

An amendment stating that nothing in the acquis communautaire shall be interpreted as challenging the right of member states to withdraw from the European Union under their own authority.

The first amendment would mean that policies including fisheries, agriculture, macroeconomic management, foreign aid, taxation policy, defence as well as many others would all be repatriated to Westminster. It would not only end the flow of directives that is saddling our economy with uncompetitive bureaucratic rules but actually at a stroke remove thousands of currently existing directives from UK law. The second amendment would require the renegotiation of the EU's protectionist customs unions and would enable the UK to join NAFTA if it so desired. The third amendment clarifies once and for all that member states have the right to secede (just as they currently have the right to leave NATO).

Conclusion: it is time to act

The more fundamental the constitutional and political issue the more essential it is to have a clear policy. The single currency is about who governs us. It is therefore part of a broader question. To concentrate all of one's efforts and time on the sole question of the Euro would do nothing to solve our fundamental problem and would be to endorse a half way house policy.

The British people are losing interest in the political process and turning against politicians because they sense that the elite has betrayed them. Fewer and fewer are turning out to vote and the membership rolls of political parties are thinning year on year. This is because the people rightly sense that the UK Parliament is increasingly irrelevant. It is time to act to recover our democracy and to campaign for a renegotiation of the Treaties.

Notes

[1] Bill Cash is the Conservative Member of Parliament for Stone and is Chairman of the European Foundation, publisher of The European Journal and the European Foundation Intelligence Digest (see www.europeanfoundation.org). He has been a senior member of the House of Commons' European Legislation Select Committee since 1985 and led parliamentary opposition to the Maastricht Treaty. He is the Vice-Chairman of the Backbench Committee on European Affairs and was Chairman 1989-91. He has written several books and pamphlets on Britain and Europe including *A Democratic Way to*

European Unity—Arguments against Federalism, 1990; *Against a Federal Europe—the Battle for Britain*, 1991; *Europe—The Crunch*, 1992; *The Blue Paper—A Response to the Government's White Paper*, 1995; *Are we really winning on Europe?*, 1996; *British and German National Interests*, 1998; and *Associated, Not Absorbed - the Associated European Area: a constructive alternative to a single European State*, 2000. He has also written many articles in *The Times, Daily Telegraph* and other newspapers and periodicals since 1986 on the subject of Europe. Bill Cash holds an MA in History from Oxford University.

[2] Chris Shore (2000), *Building Europe: the Cultural Politics of European Integration*. London: Routledge.

[3] Benedict Anderson, (1983) *Imagined Communities: reflections on the origins and spread and nationalism*. London: Verso.

[4] There is a massive critical literature on the negative economic and welfare consequences of adopting the Euro which I shall not attempt to summarise here. See for example Jean-Jacques Rosa (1998) *L'Erreur Européenne*, Paris: Grasset; Graeme Leach (2000) 'The UK and Euroland: ships passing in the night,' Policy Paper, London: Institute of Directors (available at http://www.iod.co.uk/eurouk.pdf) ; Wilhelm Nölling (2001) 'Has the Euro lived up to expectations?,' *European Journal* 8(3): 8-10, January-February; Brian Hindley (2001), 'Review of Lessons for EMU from the History of Monetary Unions' *European Journal* 8(4): 30-31.

[5] 85/511/EEC as amended, article 13(1).

[6] 85/511/EEC as amended, article 13(3).

[7] For further information see Bill Cash, MP (2000) Not Nice at All revisited, *European Foundation Working Paper 5*, London: European Foundation; Bill Cash, MP (2001) The Camouflage of Nice, *European Foundation Working Paper 6*, London: European Foundation; Allister Heath (2001) Arguments against European centralisation. *European Foundation Working Paper 7*, London: European Foundation. All three papers available on www.europeanfoundation.org/pubs/wp/index.html.

[8] *Die Welt*, 12 December 2000.

[9] *European Foundation Intelligence Digest*, 109, December 2000, London : European Foundation. Available on www.europeanfoundation.org/pubs/id/index.html.

[10] Bill Cash (2000) *Associated, Not Absorbed - the Associated European Area: a constructive alternative to a single European State*, London: European Foundation. Available on www.europeanfoundation.org/pubs/books/index.html.

[11] These amendments are based on those I suggested in Cash (2000), op. cit.

Chapter 15

A Better Britain

by Simon Buckby

Editor's Commentary

My own hope, as I put it in my Introduction, is that however the question is posed there will be a real debate and a real exploration of the options. We should not forget that the fact that both our main political parties have been divided for a number of years at different times on the European issue has had a negative effect on Britain's ability to argue for, protect and promote its interests in Brussels. I know that as a practitioner and participant. A clear outcome in the referendum should at last enable us to put behind us the disadvantage of a lack of national consensus in our approach to the EU – and the sooner the better.

Our interests have suffered, and our partners have been annoyed (and therefore less willing to accommodate us) not so much because we have been awkward customers as that we have seemed unable to make up our minds about what we want. In the EU putting forward your own ideas is usually much more likely to bring results than just saying no to others'. The latter approach, as we have seen, also brings a proliferation of negative news stories which makes the task even more difficult.

The Britain in Europe movement has the unenviable task of trying to overturn the voting forecasts and influence the timing: **Simon Buckby** *sets out the challenge and how he hopes to meet it. He deals robustly with those favouring a retreat from Europe and argues for the level playing field joining the Euro would provide. For him, being pro-European is the best way to promote the British national interest.*

A Better Britain

by Simon Buckby

An extraordinary notion has long been propagated by some opponents of Britain's place in Europe. Virtually unchecked in the quarter-century since the referendum that overwhelmingly confirmed our membership, it has now contaminated the debate about whether or not we should join the single currency. It is the idea that to be pro-European is to be anti-British and that the best way to stand up for Britain is to pull down the shutters around our borders and be at best wary of, at worst hostile to, working too closely with foreigners. Its modern incarnation runs something like this: that fourteen other countries have ganged together, largely under Franco-German leadership, to forge a European 'super-state,' of which the Euro is the final brick in the wall, that is dedicated to destroying the traditional British way of life.

Written so starkly this concept seems ludicrous. But it is reinforced almost everyday by allegations that 'Brussels bureaucrats' are plotting to deprive us of critical elements of our unique thousand years of history. This is the motive that lies behind those press stories about the European Commission apparently scheming to straighten our bananas, raise our taxes and strip us of the ability to govern ourselves. Further evidence for this fantasy comes frequently in the form of out-of-context quotations from European politicians about 'federalism,' and occasionally by menacing references to what is described as the Germanic character and history of expansionism. The corollary of this dark chain of reasoning is that for the sake of national preservation, Britain must at all costs reject the Euro and quite possibly consider withdrawal from the European Union altogether because positive engagement is self-defeating.

Not all opponents of Europe or the Euro express themselves like this. But it is the underlying thought of a vociferous group who have grabbed disproportionate space for their views in the debate. And this has so distorted the issues it has prevented reasonable people from winning a decent hearing for the case for joining the single currency.

The starting point for the vast majority of pro-Europeans is a desire to properly advance the British national interest. In the interconnected, globalised modern world, no country – not even the planet's only super-power – is able to nurture the security and prosperity of its citizens without working closely with others. Britain accepted that reality, unpleasant though it was to many, in its most fundamental form in 1949 when we admitted that alone we were unable even to defend our shores from attack, which is why we joined the Nato alliance.

The same principle applied when we belatedly entered the European Economic Community in 1973: that the legal authority vested in our sovereign – the Queen in Parliament – was no longer sufficient for our economy to grow to its fullest potential; and that therefore we would benefit from sharing some decisions with our closest trading partners to increase the power of our joint actions. This is what Winston Churchill, the embodiment of Great Power Britishness, famously and properly described as our 'larger sovereignty.'

This is the casus belli of today's anti-Europeans, who wrongly conflate national sovereignty with national survival and claim that British identity is suffocated by European integration. The simple answer to this confused thinking has been provided by the analogy of a rope: each of the fifteen members of the European Union is symbolised by a different coloured skein of silk; braided together they retain their individuality, distinct enough to be seen separately one from another, but gather in strength. This thought is at the very heart of the Treaty of Rome, in which the phrase 'ever closer union' implies proximity not merger, with members discrete as well as integrated. Failure to understand that in Europe Britain is preserving our identity while increasing our power has prevented some protagonists from honestly balancing the merits of the European Union and the Euro. Hence their arguments tend to be based on viscera or dogma rather than a rational assessment of Britain's national interests.

Britain is an island trading nation. The equivalent of about 26 per cent of our national income comes from foreign trade, compared to only 12 per cent for the United States and an average of 21 per cent for industrialised nations. This means that stability in our trading relations with our biggest trading partners is unusually central to our national prosperity.

There is no doubt which countries are our biggest trading partners these days. More than half our trade is with the other members of the European Union; in fact 57 per cent of our goods exports go to Europe, up from 35 per cent since we joined in 1973. Eight of our top ten trading partners are in the European Union, which is the leading export market for every single region and nation of the United Kingdom. The value of our goods exported to the EU is more than four times higher than to the US, we sell twice as much to Belgium as to Japan and more to France than to the entire Commonwealth.

It is because of this extraordinary level of integration that Europe is so important to us. And it is why we have devoted so much effort over nearly thirty years to overhauling protectionism and promoting free trade within Europe, first through the Common Market and then in the Single Market. Access to the Single Market, which has expanded our domestic trading area from 60 million British citizens to 370 million European consumers, has boosted our wealth substantially. Before we joined, less than £5 billion of our trade was with the rest of Europe; today that figure is £132 billion, £25 billion in services and £107 billion in goods. More than 750,000 British-based companies now trade with Europe. And there are at least 1,000 Japanese and 2,500 US companies that have come here largely as their bridgehead to export across Europe. In consequence, up to 3.5 million British jobs depend on our trading relations with Europe.

Our economy is so entwined with Europe that leaving would be devastating. In a comprehensive examination of the costs of withdrawal, the National Institute of Economic and Social Research concluded that if we were denied access to the Single Market and trade barriers were re-introduced, as many of them undoubtedly would be, then they would raise the effective price of our exports by around 9 per cent. This would inevitably result in the relocation of so many foreign firms to other countries within the Single Market that our stock of inward investment might be cut by up to one-third in manufacturing. In fact, when the likely impact of leaving was run through the NIESR economic model, it calculated that after two decades the volume of our output would be 2 per cent lower than might otherwise have been sustained; it also estimated that our real gross national income would be 1.5 per cent down and our household consumption 2.5 per cent less than might otherwise have been the case. Quite simply, outside we would all be poorer.

Our country would be weaker too. Without influence over critical decisions that increasingly affect our destiny, whether we like it or not, our economy would be further beholden to events beyond our control. Nor would we be so well placed to work with our neighbours to address other problems that transcend national borders, from deterring international criminals to cutting environmental pollution.

Anti-Europeans sometimes suggest that we should retreat from the European Union and settle in the European Economic Area, which they hold up as the model of a free trade association. They contend that we should copy Norway in negotiating access to the Single Market, winning all the benefits of free trade but avoiding all the political implications of the European Union's Council of Ministers, Commission and Parliament. However, they overlook the fact that in return for this access, Norway is compelled to implement the entire apparatus of EU law, enforced by the European Court of Justice, while having no say whatsoever in its formulation. This position can hardly be said to maintain national sovereignty.

Anti-Europeans also trumpet the North American Free Trade Agreement, where they say we could improve our relations with the United States, Canada and Mexico. But because the European Commission is responsible for the trade policy of all European Union member countries – and is negotiating free trade deals between the EU and NAFTA – it would not be possible for us to unilaterally join NAFTA without also leaving the EU. Given that less than 5 per cent of US trade is with Britain, most of which is already tariff free, and that Britain conducts almost four times as much trade with the EU as with NAFTA, it would put ideological dogma over economic sanity to leave one for the other.

Exiting Europe would reduce our clout in the world too. With our historic global reach Britain is the entry point to Europe for countries around the earth, not least because of our special relationship with the United States and our leadership of the Commonwealth. Far from being in conflict, these unique relations are bolstered by each other and to sacrifice any one of them would inevitably weaken the other two. We are a bridge to the world precisely because we are a gateway to Europe. Britain is stronger and richer in Europe and in the right conditions we would be even better off in the Euro. Joining the Euro would be the logical extension of the decision we took to enter Europe; rejecting the single currency would be tantamount to unlearning the lessons of history and reversing nearly thirty years of consistent economic and foreign policy.

The debate about the single currency in Britain often seems stuck in a time warp. It is no longer sufficient to consider whether or not Economic and Monetary Union is desirable: that argument raged in the years from the Delors Report in 1989 to the Maastricht Treaty in 1991 to the launch of the Euro in 1999. It is now necessary to examine the consequences of Britain signing up to or staying out of a system that is already used by twelve of our major trading partners in our primary trading association. We might feel that we are taking stock, but in fact we are being left behind because our leading competitors are stealing a march on us by sharing a common currency.

The Common Market stimulated trade by removing tariffs and duties. The Single Market created the single largest consumer market in the world by abolishing or harmonising regulations, so freeing the movement of people and capital, goods and services. The single currency is designed to complete the Single Market by circumventing the costs of currency transactions and the risks of exchange movements, which are just as much a barrier to trade as tariffs and regulations.

Apart from the obvious costs of changing money from one currency to another – which the CBI estimates is a burden on British business to the tune of 0.4 per cent of GDP or £3.6 billion a year – the real problem for those exposed to foreign trade is the prospect of continual changes in the relative values of currencies. With freely floating exchange rates, the profitability of all businesses that export abroad or compete against imports at home partly depends on the value of the currency: too high a rate leads to a loss of competitiveness and eventually to redundancies and bankruptcies, too low a rate makes imports expensive and nourishes inflation, and repeated shifts from high to low and back again hamper business planning and inject instability into the economy. Some protection can be afforded against the risk of currency fluctuations by hedging in the forward exchange markets, commonly through futures contracts, but they are very costly and usually limited to short time periods. As it is not possible to insure fully, the possibility of currency gyrations deters long-term investment and hinders medium-sized enterprises from expanding abroad. In reality, sudden changes in the exchange rate can cut margins at a stroke, and in the long-term profits can be wiped out completely.

This has always been a particular difficulty for Britain for two reasons. First, because sterling has a terrible record of volatility, see-sawing in value in the short-term as well as depreciating in the long-term against the other major currencies, the deutschmark, the dollar and the yen. Second, because such a large proportion of our wealth is dependent on foreign trade, currency movements have had a disproportionate impact on the performance of our economy. But the problem has worsened severely now that so much of our trade is concentrated on a single currency zone. Before the advent of the Euro, at least the risk was spread because movements between say the pound and the deutschmark did not affect British trade with France; now our national prosperity is unusually dependent on the relationship between the pound and the Euro, which has therefore become far more important to us than the dollar or the yen.

By sharing the same currency our principal competitors have internalised the vast majority of their trade, dramatically cutting their exposure to the vagaries of exchange rate movements. Exports outside the eurozone are now equivalent to just over 10 per cent of its GDP, similar to those of the US, whereas previously those of France and Germany to all other countries were equal to nearly 30 per cent each, similar to those of Britain. By abolishing the costs and risks associated with so much of their foreign trade, these countries have all leaped ahead of Britain, which has been left at a unique competitive disadvantage.

This is why British exporters and foreign investors into Britain have taken the unusual step of publicly intervening in the argument, demanding that we join the Euro as soon as the conditions allow. If we do not, especially as the high pound makes our products so expensive in the eurozone, either they will have their margins squeezed or they will relocate abroad. Either way, competitiveness, investment and jobs are all at risk.

In fact, despite the relatively good shape that our economy is in, there has already been severe damage. During the first year of the Euro our share of new projects from foreign investment into Europe fell from 28 per cent to 24 per cent while the French share jumped from 12 per cent to 18 per cent. And since the Euro was launched companies have publicly blamed our exclusion for an average of 3,500 British job losses every single month. If our economy were less robust, or if it became clear that our repudiation were permanent, the pain would be much greater still.

By denying ourselves a level playing field, staying out would clearly mean losing out. Actively choosing not to join, or even continuing to defer a conscious decision, would certainly lead to a number of high profile casualties, adding to those of Rover at Longbridge, Ford at Dagenham and Vauxhall at Luton in the motor manufacturing sector alone in the recent past. But it is unlikely that there would be a sudden economic disaster, a massive collapse in trade or a huge hike in unemployment. Although some sectors would obviously suffer immediately, especially in manufacturing, for a few years our economy might be able to carry on as if little had changed. Gradually, however, perhaps almost imperceptibly, we would fail to fulfil our economic potential and start to slip behind our European rivals, with slower growth rates than theirs and more job losses than we would otherwise have had. After all, we have been in that boat before: it is exactly what happened when we spurned the European Coal and Steel Community in 1952 and the European Economic Community in 1957 until harsh reality finally drove us in.

The economic case for joining in the right conditions is overwhelmingly powerful. It would be better for Britain. It would be better for business because trade and investment would rise, and it would be better for workers because jobs would be safe and secure. Furthermore, it would be better for shoppers because transparency would drive prices down and it would be better for homeowners because the historic lower interest rates in Europe would make mortgages cheaper. Above all, it would be better for our economy because it would guarantee stability and prevent the return of boom and bust. Yet these economic benefits are often overlooked out of fear of the political implications, notably the supposed sanctity of national sovereignty.

Yet far from standing up for Britain, these fearmongers are in fact letting Britain down. By refusing to address the issue on its merits, they would have Britain make the wrong choices for ideological reasons: in the long-term Britain would be much worse off outside the Euro so their defence of national sovereignty is illusory. The genuine patriot does not look first to harbour our sovereignty, but at how it can best be deployed to advance the interests of our country. For the public to vote for the Euro, therefore, the debate about Europe in Britain needs to revolve around an entirely different axis to that dictated by anti-Europeans in recent years. To be pro-European is not to be anti-British. Quite the reverse. We are only pro-European because we want to build a better Britain.

Chapter 16

'You've got to be in to influence'

Neil Kinnock

Editor's Commentary

I have tried as editor to provide a balanced platform for all the principal thrusts of argument on the Euro issue; I am only sorry, if any reader feels one strand or another is missing, that not all those whom the Federal Trust or I invited to contribute wished to accept.

*Editorially, we took the decision to invite contributions only from those directly involved in British politics, although we wished to extend that interpretation to include British MEPs, since they are after all elected to represent British views in Brussels and Strasbourg. We did however want to conclude this collection with a view from Brussels, and thought that, particularly as we assume it will be under a Labour government that a referendum is held, **Neil Kinnock** would be the ideal person to offer the final contribution, which he agreed to do in an interview with me as editor in late July, after all the contributions were in.*

As someone whose personal views on Britain and Europe (which I hope have not intruded on the contents of this book) have not changed fundamentally with time, indeed have been reinforced by experience, I am bound to salute those who have maintained the same position, whether for or against, over time. I have however to confess to a particular admiration for those whose views have been affected by what the Russians used to call Life Itself. Neil Kinnock is one such, and I am particularly pleased that he closes this volume and am grateful to him for doing so. One of his messages is the need to explain and communicate: we have tried to do so in this book.

'You've got to be in to influence'

Neil Kinnock

interviewed by Roger Beetham

Why in your view do we need EMU and the single currency – is it necessary because of the single market? NK: Yes, I'm one of the people who believes that single markets beget single currencies simply because of the realties of efficiency. The currency is obviously the means of exchange and if there are different, divergent currencies inside the place of exchange- the single market – it's an inhibition to the single market and it limits the cost reductions and other advantages which the single market makes possible. The existence of a single market is a substantial reason for both the existence of and the need for a single currency.

Do you see that in primary European terms, or do you envisage a world role for the Euro? NK: The prime reason for the existence of the Euro obviously does not originate from global market considerations. The reality is, however, that- in addition to the European and single market arguments for a single currency – the advent of the Euro provides the world with a necessary choice of trading currencies. The Euro, which has as its base one of the most prosperous parts of the world, is bound to become a world currency – it would even without the scale of global market integration that we've got now. With the current level of global market integration, it's a certainty and a necessity.

It's going to be very difficult, in the short term, to manage the transition. Have you, living in Euroland started to think in Euros yet? NK: I tend to translate prices into Euros. When the Euro rate is a nice neat figure like about 60 pence it's very easy to do. Other figures are more awkward of course- but you always work out a neat, quick formula!

Do you think it's a good idea that the transition period, where national currencies and the Euro circulate together, has been drastically reduced, from six months to six weeks? NK: Yes, absolutely. It can generate some irritation in the short term and the potential of inconvenience in the early months is certain – in an age of slot machines and other mechanical transaction facilities some things are bound to go wrong. But there's no practical point in hanging about for several months.

Turning now to Britain, the majority of contributors to this book, and I myself, feel the decision whether or not to join the single currency is primarily a political one, although of course the economic tests, particularly on convergence and timing, must be met. How far do you feel joining is an economic decision or a political one? NK: My own view has always been that this is fundamentally an economic decision with major political implications. The major political implication is that the United Kingdom will not exercise its fully justified influence on European Union political affairs if its absence from the Euro is prolonged. If the prospect of absence from the Euro stretched ahead for many years our essential, entirely necessary, political influence would be diminished.

Has that process started, with the continuing uncertainty in Britain? NK: I don't think so – but mainly because of reasons that haven't got much to do with the Euro. It's fortunate that we have a British government that is very evidently pro-EU, so there is no sense of alienation between members of the government and colleagues in any other governments or indeed any EU institutions. Secondly, the Labour government has a huge mandate so there's an understanding that people are not dealing with a weak or fragile government. Thirdly, there is a swirl of political events from enlargement to the Middle East, from the globalised economy to Kyoto which ensure that the government of the UK, a substantial and wealthy economy, is directly engaged. So, any idea of exclusion or marginal of Britain would just be silly.

This is why in considering the Euro I put an emphasis on the medium to longer term. If the impression was gained that Britain's absence from the eurozone was to be prolonged there would be two effects. Firstly, a gradual erosion of necessary influence in the conduct of affairs in the European Union not because anybody would seek to exclude but simply because the United Kingdom would not be there at the centre of economic decisions. Secondly, if business and commerce gathered the impression that Britain was going to be absent form the Euro for a prolonged period it would simply change the economic environment. In terms of confidence and investment commitment to Britain the consequences of that would be entirely disadvantageous. Even the most rooted Europhobe could not count up advantages of prolonged absence.

Has the size of Labour's election victory increased expectations and therefore made it more difficult to play on without a clear decision? NK: I think expectations have increased for two reasons. One is the recent event of a very large majority gained at the expense of a manifestly europhobic Conservative Party. That result might not have said precisely what the British people do want, but it is said very clearly what they don't want. The other ingredient of the increase in expectation was the very explicit statement made by the Prime Minister in March about undertaking the two year analysis with a view to coming to a recommendation at the end of it. That is understood to be a specific timetable.

Do you feel there will be a qualitative change in this complex of things you've just discussed if a decision were not taken in this Parliament? NK: There would be a significant impact on the economic environment if it became evident that there was a deliberate choice not to seek to hold a referendum in this Parliament, or if events had taken such a decision out of the hands of government. It is difficult to see circumstances in which the reality of not having a referendum in this Parliament would not have an effect on confidence, given the way in which large and small companies will be thinking, planning in, investing in, trading Euros.

So you're thinking particularly of the issues of investment in Britain? NK: Yes, because if the impression is gathered that the absence from the Euro is going to stretch over several years the impact on current and potential investors, on traders, on potential employers, manufactures, providers of services would be salutary. They would have to say that the 'major factor in our medium and long-term calculations is going to be the location that we have and the nature of our access to our major market – the rest of the European Union. If none of our competitors is going to have to pay an exchange rate premium or transaction costs but we will have to, and if our currency is overvalued because we are outside the Euro that's a real bump on the nose. We can't take too many of those, and we won't either.' Naturally, I would try to persuade them not to take a negative attitude towards undertaking future development in the United Kingdom. I think it would be something of a struggle, however.

One argument which is difficult to deal with is, after the Irish experience particularly, that the single currency is a straitjacket and one model for

all doesn't work. NK: There are two points. Firstly, in the United Kingdom and most other largish economies we've always been in 'a one size fits all' monetary policy.

In our national single market the interest rate regime has always been operated by the government and the Bank to deal with the most heated parts of the economy, never to deal with the flattest parts of the economy. That interest rate regime has often had an arresting effect in the most prosperous parts of the economy and a depressive effect elsewhere-but no one has ever said 'let's have a discriminatory interest rate,' and they've been right not to be so unrealistic. Second, there is similar history with fiscal policy. Relative tightness of policy has often directly contradicted the budgetary needs of substantial parts of the United Kingdom but nobody has said 'let's have differentiated budgetary policy.' Of course, the regional development policies that we've had since the 1930's have provided some compensation- but never so much that it made a gigantic difference. So the European monetary union has not invented a one size fits all interest rate and budgetary regime. We've always lived with it just as they have in Germany or France or Italy.

On the issue of Commission comments on the Irish budget; we followed the procedure of the Stability and Growth pact (which Ireland has agreed) and we submitted our assessment. Why did Ireland agree to the system of Commission reports in the first place? Because the country and the government realised that the advantages of being in a zone of currency stability are much bigger than any possible disadvantages that come form a regime of recommendation and examination that promotes stability and sustainable growth. In the short term I understand why national politicians say 'How dare they look over our shoulder.' But I don't think Ireland would be saying that if the country about which we were making budgetary strategy recommendations was, for example, Germany. Analysis and recommendation by the Commission, and debate and decision by the Council, is the realistic and agreed requirement of a single currency regime that has got much more advantages than disadvantages.

Of course, if people want to ensure that the 'one size' takes proper account of the need to fit UK realities they should advocate joining the Euro. Our country will be very directly affected by its use by all of our neighbours and in our main markets so it will make sense for the UK to exercise all possible influence on the economic policies relating to the currency.

A fear has been expressed that the Commission will be bureaucratic and insist that sterling spend two years in the ERM before joining the Euro. NK: Clearly it's in the United Kingdom's interest to be absolutely certain that there's sufficient alignment and that the requirements that would arise out of participation in the monetary system are met. But the idea that when alignment is clearly evident there would be an effort to lock the UK out for two years in order to go through a formal process is not politically or economically realistic.

What is it about your time Brussels that has really marked your views of the European process? NK: I always made the argument that the idea that there was some rampant pursuit of centralised political union was unreal. The closer I have got to decision making, the more certain I am that such ambitions do not exist in the mind of any significant think-tanker, civil servant, representative of a politician or anybody. I think that we should be more assertive in telling that truth.

How then do you overcome the feeling in the minds of British people that talk of moving towards closer European Union inevitably means a superstate? NK: To adapt a phrase - 'explanation, explanation, explanation.' The European Institutions, member-state governments, the media (even the media that wants to explain) do an awful job of informing. People are not going to accept a declaratory reassurance that there is going to be no superstate no matter how true it happens to be. They are not going to be reassured, let alone confident, without having some more basic information about what the European Union does, why it exists, how it does what it does, how well it does what it does, how much money it has (or how little), how it spends the money, who spends the money, who are they responsible to, and also what is important apart from the money. It's an hour-long chat, it's not rocket science. And it's never really been done on a sufficient scale. Now it has to be. The truth is that the Union is not going to be a State of any kind. And the claims that it will be must be actively demolished, not airily dismissed.

Do you feel that the Commission understands that with enlargement in particular there's quite enough going on without pushing ahead in too many fields? NK: Absolutely. When you come to think of it, this Commission has quite a remarkable set of tasks. We're very lucky - we're the first generation in history to have the absolute guarantee that there will be no general conflict in this continent. Even where horrendous local conflicts (mainly ethnic rivalries) explode, they're now less likely to do so than ever in history. I'm one of those who feels that the great venture of enlargement, together with further CAP reform in 2002, the maturing of EMU, modernisation of the Commission, and pursuit of other active strategies in, for instance, the single market, trade, transport, environment, food safety, justice and home affairs all give us a very full and useful workload. Piling up other tasks might be good for the ego- but it won't do anything for real output.

The British are particularly concerned about accountability, the famous democratic deficit. Everyone was terribly excited about the first direct elections to the European Parliament in 1979, but I think your wife, as an MEP, would agree that it has been a great disappointment and it's not the only way to fill the democratic deficit. NK: I think that Glenys' and my view are about the same: Where the European Parliament works as an analysing, advocating, advising, revising body it can be bloody good. Many of the Parliamentarians there are as capable as you'll find anywhere.

So, it can do a better job of making its contribution to closing the democratic deficit if it performs to the best of its ability and powers. Now, that might mean that the role is rather more humble in the short and medium than some people would like but in parliamentary terms of course a better job is being done.

I must say that I think that the problem is more to do with an information and a comprehension deficit than a real democratic deficit. If there is a lack of belief in the connection between the individual voter and the parliament, the only way to reduce that is for people to understand how the parliament came about, what it does and how it does it. There is hardly any public comprehension of that. I don't think that's the fault of the citizen: I think that there's a complete lack of effort from the media to do anything but treat the European Parliament with scorn, and secondly I think that the Parliament could and should do a much better job of explaining what it does and how it does it for itself. That's part of the raw task of any Parliament.

Do you think changing the system in Britain has had a negative effect, for example on voter participation? NK: I'm in favour of PR but I think that the system chosen for the Euro elections was the wrong system. They could've kept those big constituencies. In many cases they were real constituencies where electors had a real idea of who their representative was. If they kept the system of 84 constituencies and introduced a more proportionally organised single-member election I think we would have had a bigger turnout and much more comprehension. The awful thing is that, just as people were getting used to the idea of having a Member of the European parliament, they were confronted by regional representation with MEP's from four or five parties. I think that the Regional List is a step backwards from the constituency system previously used.

Is there anything on your side of the channel that the member states or the Commission could do to help understanding of the issues in the run-up to a referendum-without of course intervening directly? NK: I think the best thing that can be done, not just in the case of the Euro but in the appraisal and understanding of the European Union generally, is to make a full-hearted commitment to explanation. That will certainly help with de-mystifying and de-demonising the European Union in the United Kingdom. But, since reservation about the European Union is not a British monopoly, I think it's necessary to be done generally. I also think as political parties and governments must come to realise that misunderstandings about, or lack of comprehension of, the European Union and their country's place in it are political realities with increasing domestic impact. It is therefore in the interest of national governments and political parties to stop taking people for granted over commitment to the European Union, and engage systematically in some better explanation as part of their domestic campaigning. I regret that it has to be done when we've been in for 28 years-but really would welcome some extra effort.

What do you say to those who are not ready to decide and to those who have not firmly made up their minds? NK: I would simply say for the sake of the United Kingdom and the sake of the European generation of which we are part, Britain should take a lead. Doing so is a marvellous mix of self-interest and general interest.

Everyone should understand the reality: To exercise influence you've got to be in. There is no such thing as outfluence.